D1027397

For "Charley Girl"– a friend and an inspiration...
And Joyce, Charley's "Mom"

Forward to the Second Edition

In 2017 I published "Walks with Charley". It was my first experience in publishing with a professional publisher. I learned a lot by going through the process with professionals, particularly all the issues about use, ownership, copyright, and permissions related to publishing images.

Yet, after the book was published, there were things I wanted to fix, most importantly, portrayal of images which add richness and understanding to any discussion and comments. When first published I was forced into a picture limit that ended with a creation of a composite figure at the end of each chapter that rendered many images unreadable.

Also, I received suggestions for additional stories, by email, letter, and face-to-face.

This edition addresses the suggestions and fixes that I consider errors – and it makes me happier.

Also, several new stories, mostly about "Green Valley" were added, so the book grew in size by about 35%.

Table of Contents and Figures

Preface

Arlington, Virginia, is a county with many communities, public parks and memorial areas. Much of the area is famous worldwide for the notable the Pentagon, Arlington Cemetery, and Reagan National Airport.

There are many histories written along with picture volumes that document much of the area's history. Most of those histories have been oriented on North Arlington. Up until the late 1900's, South Arlington had a mostly unremarkable history from a sparsely populated farmland, seedy locales outside the Nation's Capital, to an industrial area.

I found, after reading nearly all the popular books about Arlington, that there was very little about South Arlington, and even less about the area I had called home since 1990, Arlington Ridge. The fact that I met my wife and was married in Arlington in the early 1960's and had lived in the area several times didn't add anything to my knowledge of the ground underneath my feet.

The composite map (Figure 1) [1] depicts all of Arlington County with shaded areas identifying the various community associations.

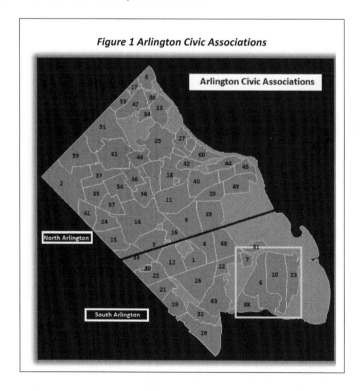

Figure 1 Arlington Civic Associations

This book is mostly about the area within the yellow rectangle, with the following Arlington Ridge civic associations: 6-Arlington Ridge Civic Association (ARCA);

7-Arlington View; 10-Aurora Highlands Civic Association (AHCA) which represents the Virginia Highlands, Addison Heights and Aurora Hills subdivisions; 23-Crystal City; and 38-Long Branch Creek area that includes the large Gunston School and the Park and Arna Valley (now Avalon) properties.

The Arlington Ridge area ("the Ridge") is currently defined by the geographic high ground bordered on the north and west by Shirley Highway, and bordered on the south by South Glebe Road and east by South Eads Street.

Figure 2 is an extract of an 1878 map with the black oval circumscribing the Arlington Ridge area [2]. The diagonal, unimproved road with "Addison" near the center is today's Arlington Ridge Road. The Pentagon would be located in the upper left cormer of the figure.

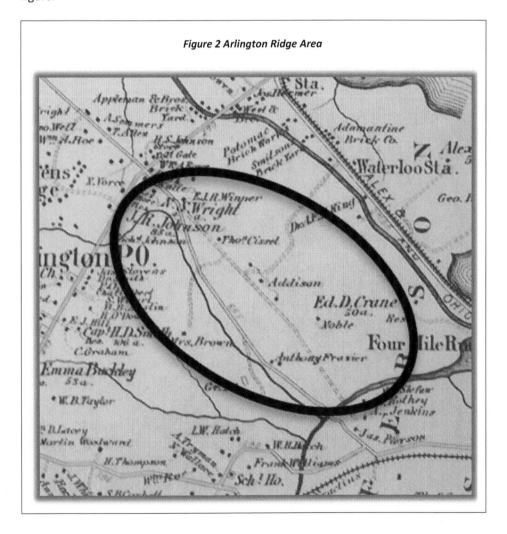

Figure 2 Arlington Ridge Area

I am not a historian nor am I a history writer. Even though I did well in history in school, my memories about it are unmemorable. I think part of not remembering much is simply the way history had to be written and learned – a chronological recitation of facts and dates not necessarily with some context a student can have personal interest in. I thought assembling a collection of short, memoir-type stories based on personal experience, even if I didn't live during original historical events, might be more interesting, and more memorable – at least to me.

Thus, I have written about Arlington Ridge in terms of personal explorations by my "best friend" Charley and me. When you walk a dog several miles a day in the same general area you encounter many things that are missed when you are alone, just walking or driving a car. With a dog, you must stop and attend to the "duties" of the dog. The shared journey is the important thing, not getting somewhere. You must stop and wait for "sniffing" expeditions. And you (the human) can share your observations and wonder with someone (the dog) who is non-judgmental.

Since Charley and I daily traverse much of the area we are also a "strobe light" on change. We report downed trees to the county. We observe poor workmanship and repairs. And, even though we may have passed a location hundreds of times, we may see something new, even things as large as houses.

Thus, I have tried to create a series of "readers digestible" stories (a made-up term for a story quickly read and easily understood) that relate the here and now to yesteryear with the help of Charley.

This book is organized by first introducing you, the reader, to Charley, then by working our way around the Ridge geographically. If north is at 12 o'clock, that is where I start and work clockwise and back to 12 o'clock.

I hope you will enjoy my shared journey and experiences with Charley as much as I have. Charley doesn't remember any of the story details (unless there are smells involved), but she does remember her way around the nearly twenty miles of roads, alleys, and paths of the Ridge.

Date written: 9/6/2016 revised 12/30/2019

Charley Girl

Joyce and I had dogs most of our married life. When Shu, our last Shih Tzu went to doggie heaven, we decided not to get another dog. Our lifestyle had not changed enough to be keeping and training a puppy – it didn't fit.

On the other hand, I loved the idea of "unconditional love" not available anywhere else, but from a dog.

When Joyce retired in 2009, we could begin to see a chance for unconditional love – again.

We settled on getting a Wheaton Terrier-Shih Tzu mix, Abbey. We paid a breeder a lot of money for her and had a training package built in. She was cute and sweet but was un-trainable in terms of house breaking. Maybe we were out of practice. We tried everything, but ultimately had to take her to Animal Welfare League. She was picked up immediately and we were led to believe she was placed with a family who could do the right thing. All in all, it was a sad experience.

After two years, and still in need of unconditional love, Joyce began searching the Internet. Joyce wanted a dog that could be trained as a therapy dog for working with children in reading programs. I wasn't particularly interested, but the idea of unconditional love was still appealing.

In January 2010 Joyce asked me to come with her to Winchester. We would see some puppies, but, "...only to look". [3]

Figure 3 Charley as Puppy -- 3 Months

Figure 4 Pickup from Breeder -- 3 Months

A little white Goldendoodle puppy crawled into my lap and it was love at first sight (figure 3). I kept saying we weren't committing, but I had her picture on my phone and I kept looking at it.

We were going to Monterey, California in early February and Tucson, Arizona in March, and we decided to commit to take the dog if the breeder was willing to keep her until we returned. We didn't think it was fair to pick her up then put her in a kennel right away. The breeder agreed. She was the favorite of the litter and the breeder had named her "Lamb Chop" after the Sherri Lewis puppet of the same name. While in Monterrey we visited the Steinbeck Museum and that sealed the fate of her name, Charley. Recall Steinbeck's last book was "Travels with Charley".

When we picked her up in April, it was still love at first sight only enhanced by the fact that she was completely housebroken and proved that skill just before we left the breeder (figure 4).

Now nearly nine years later, Charley is mid-sized (50 pounds – nearly the same weight she was at 6 months) and always gets comments, when we walk, "...she is so beautiful...", "...she always looks just groomed...", and when petted by children, "...she is so soft and fluffy..." (figure 5). All those attributes are hers, naturally. She is beautiful, sweet, gentle, and very fit – she makes sure I get my daily exercise, often 6-8 miles -- every day in an "unconditional" way.

Figure 5 Charley on Her "Perch" on Back Deck --6 Months

Date written: 1/28/2015 revised 12/30/2019

What's in a name of a place? How did that name get decided? Whose life is now immortalized.

The story of the names of places can represent a fascinating tale about the place where we live, yet often, know little about.

From 2001 to 2018 we lived on South Nash Street in Arlington, Virginia. South Nash is located on the area generally described as Arlington Ridge, a topographic "finger" that points to Arlington House, the Lee mansion in Arlington Cemetery, through the area of the Pentagon. In the 1800's Anthony Fraser and James Roach owned the properties. Today, the following streets, clockwise from the north, bound the area: S. Joyce St, S. Glebe Road, and Army Navy Drive. Over time, parts of the area have been known as: Green Valley, Club Manor Estates, Aurora Hills, Addison Heights, Virginia Highlands, and Aurora Highlands -- all very confusing to outsiders and residents alike.

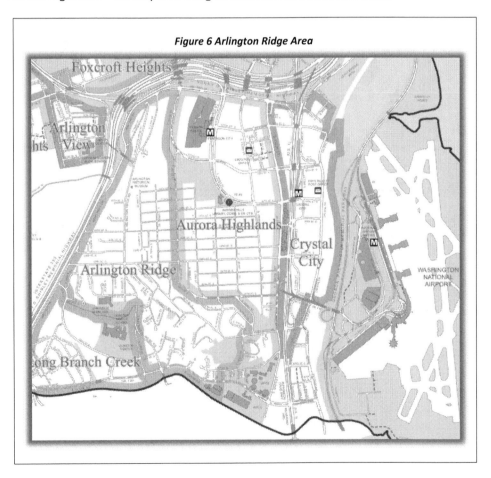

Figure 6 Arlington Ridge Area

Most of the paved roadways in the immediate surroundings of South Nash Street are less than 100 years old. Though some roads date back to the Revolution, most have new names. South Nash is also a switchback extension of Arlington Ridge Road leading downhill from the Pentagon overlook to Army-Navy Drive (figure 6)[4].

So, what is the evolution on of the name Arlington Ridge?

Much of the area was once part of the 1,000-acre estate of Anthony Fraser. The area was known as Green Valley, likely named for James Green, who lived on the land near the present location of the clubhouse at Army Navy Country Club. Fraser acquired the land from a family by the name of Alexander. It straddled lower Long Branch stream, a tributary of Four Mile Run. The Fraser estate included what is now the Army-Navy Country Club, Oakridge Elementary School, Gunston Middle School, Shirley Park and Arna Valley as well as land from Pentagon City and the River Houses to the banks of Four Mile Run.

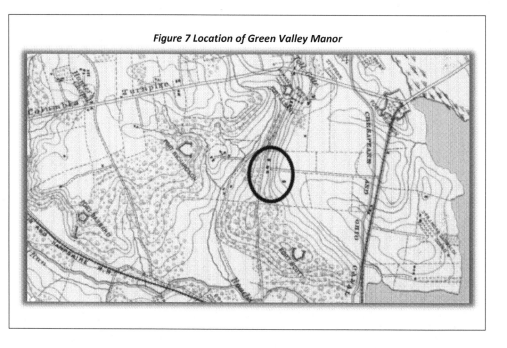

Figure 7 Location of Green Valley Manor

In 1821 Anthony Fraser (sometimes spelled Frazier) built a home and named it Green Valley Manor (figures 7[5] & 8[6]). It was located in the floor of a valley about a hundred yards from Long Branch, near the intersection of the current South Queen Street (in the Forest Hills townhouse development) and South 23th Street (formerly Fraser Road).

The structure was destroyed by fire in 1924 and never rebuilt. Anthony Fraser's daughter married J.E. Sickles and inherited the property.[7] After the fire she lived in the servants' house for several years.

Figure 8 Green Valley Manor

By 1840, the nearest neighbors to the Frasers were James Roach and his family. Their home was on Hoe Hill, which they renamed Prospect Hill, at the northern end of the current Arlington Ridge Road, overlooking the Pentagon.

From 1840 to 1966 Arlington Ridge Road was a single street across Arlington. The northern road began at North 19th Street and proceeded south along what is now Wilson Boulevard to Lee Boulevard (now known as Arlington Boulevard). As it proceeded south it incorporated a portion of what was informally known as Oil Plant Road (also known as "Oil Road"). In the 1960's, after the closure of the central portion when interchanges and connections for the Theodore Roosevelt Bridge were constructed, North Arlington Ridge Road was eliminated leaving the remaining South Arlington Ridge Road. By this time, it was a divided two-lane road with nearby trolley line. Residents petitioned the County in the 1960's to remove the divider and restrict travel to two lanes, and, after a trial period, it was agreed to do so. [8]

In 1890's, subdivisions with streets for the area were laid out. The first subdivision, Addison Heights, had its origin in the Addison house that appeared on maps dated 1864 and 1878, on Arlington Ridge. The house was located on the southeast corner of Arlington Ridge Road and what is today's South 20th Street. This area included 16th Street South (originally Clements Avenue) at the north end, South Fern Street (originally Cheston Avenue) at the east end, 23rd Street South (originally Fraser Avenue) at the south end, and South Arlington Ridge Road (originally Mount Vernon Avenue) at the west end. [9]

The area was primarily agricultural until the 1920's. A 1926 map of the area shows six houses between the Hume School and 20th Street. One more house existed between the school and Prospect Hill, one on the west side of the road, and a few more at the base of the Ridge on what was then Old Georgetown Road (now is part of Army-Navy Drive).

Aurora Highlands was formed by the integration of three subdivisions platted between 1896 and 1930 and included construction of single-family residences. The name Aurora Highlands comes from an amalgamation of the original three subdivisions: Addison Heights, Aurora Hills, and Virginia Highlands.

While all this development was occurring, the county changed names. In 1920, the area known as Alexandria County was divided and renamed Arlington County and the City of Alexandria.

The US Postal Service refused to establish a Post Office in Arlington until it developed an acceptable street naming and numbering scheme. In 1932 the old magisterial districts, established in 1870, were abolished, and an integrated County government was created – and names changed, including, historically significant names! The Arlington County Virginia Directory of Street Names, revised June 1, 1935 catalogs the name changes, although there are numerous errors in it, particularly for "old names".

Arlington has many places named after world-famous people, Presidents, Generals, and others of note. It also has numbered streets that replaced names of significance and thereby a loss of historical reference.

The 1932, the county changed the current street naming scheme dividing it into two sections, North and South Arlington, generally separated by Arlington Boulevard. Numbered streets generally run east west, parallel to Arlington Boulevard, and named streets generally run north south, with "North" and "South" designations preceding named street names and after numbered street names. Street names, increase in syllables as a function of distance from the Potomac River, called "iterations". The first-tier names, all within Arlington Ridge area, are one syllable. These streets are generally in alphabetical order from east to west, skipping the letters X, Y, and Z. When the end of the alphabet was reached, it is repeated with additional syllables– thus Eads, Fern, Grant, Hayes, Inge, Ives, Joyce, June, Kent, Knoll, Lynn, Nash, Ode, Pierce, Rolfe, and Queen are east of each other. Most of the boulevards, drives, and roads with historically recognized names, were not renamed (e.g., Oakcrest Road, Fort Scott Drive, Arlington Ridge Road). Generally, these are the only through streets. Numbered and named streets tend to be broken up at times and are intended for local neighborhood traffic [10] [11]. Figure 9 summarizes Arlington Ridge area name changes (next page): [12]

Figure 9 Arlington Ridge Area Name Changes (Landmarks, Streets., and Parks) From North to South

Current Name	Former Name(s) Prior to 1935	Comment/Note
Army-Navy Drive	Old Georgetown Road	Takes its present name as an access road to Army Navy Country Club, established in 1924.
S. Arlington Ridge Road	Mount Vernon Road	
Prospect Park, (S. Nash St)		Named for Prospect Hill, the 1800's home of James Roach at the site.
Hume School (S. Arlington Ridge Road)		Named for Frank Hume, a confederate veteran
S. Eads Street	Jefferson St. & Franklin Avenue	Named for civil engineer, James Buchanan Eads, 1820-1887[1]
S. Glebe Road	Glebe Road & Brookdale Avenue	A glebe was a rectory on farmland for a Church of England minister.
S. Grant	Hume Avenue, Monroe Avenue	Named for President Grant
S. Grove Street		No former name
S. Hayes	Hennigan Avenue, Tyler Avenue	Named for President Hayes
S. Ives Street	Mason Avenue	
S. Joyce Street	Willow Street and Washington Street	
S. Kent Street	Norman Street	
S. Knoll Street		No former name
S. Lynn Street	Arlington Avenue, Oakcrest	
S. 19th Road		
S. 19th Street	Girault Avenue, Prospect Street	
S. 20th Street	Addison Avenue	
S. 21st Street	Graham Street	
S. 22d Street	Gordon Street	
S. 23rd Road	Woodlawn Place	Road was never developed, just drawn on plans.
S. 23rd Road	Fraser Avenue	Named for 1800's property owner, Anthony Fraser
S. 24th Street	South Stratford Drive, Warren Avenue	
Nina Park (24th Street)		
S. 25sh Street	Green Avenue	
S. 26th Street	Washington Avenue	
S. 27th Street	Crest Avenue	
S. 28th Street	Valley Avenue, Hillside Road, Fort Scott Drive	
Fraser Park, (S. 28th Street)		Named for 1800's property owner, Anthony Fraser, (Cemetery near Hole 8, Blue course, ANCC)
Haley Park, (S. Meade Street)		Named for property owner James W. Haley
S. Meade Street	Carter's Lane	Named for Union General Meade
S. Pierce Street	Valle Road	Named for President Pierce
S. Fort Scott		Named for General Winfield Scott, then General-in-Chief of the Army
S. Ode Court	Westover Road	Westover Road was never developed, just drawn on plans; S. Ode name inherited the name from N. Ode Street
S. Nash Street	Forest Street	Inherited the name from N. Nash Street
S. Rolfe Street		Inherited the name from N. Rolfe Street
S. Queen Street	Curtis-Lee Parkway	Road was never developed, just drawn on plans.
Fort Scott Park, (Fort Scott Drive)		Named for the Civil War fort that honored General Scott.

Figure 10 (area west of Arlington Ridge Road and south of 23rd Street) was extracted from Sanborn Fire Insurance Maps for 1935 and superimposed on a current map.

The shaded portion had been built by 1935 and the non-shaded portions were planned at that time. The map also shows Fraser [Frazier] Avenue (now 23rd Street) leading to the Fraser cemetery on the Army Navy Country Club property. [13]

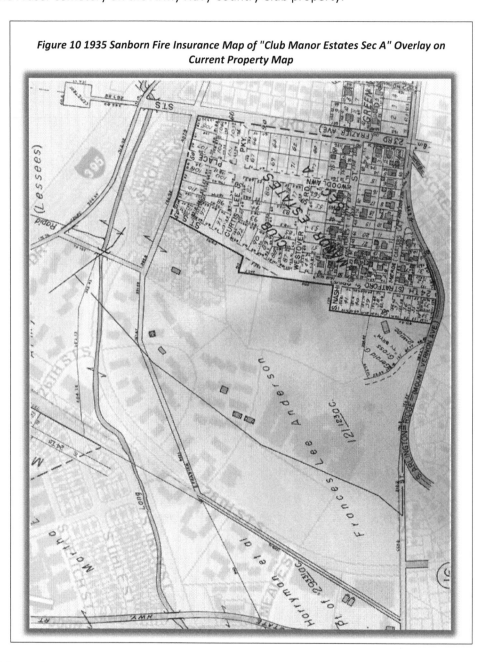

Figure 10 1935 Sanborn Fire Insurance Map of "Club Manor Estates Sec A" Overlay on Current Property Map

Where this journey started was the search for the origin of "Nash", but it expanded to whole of Arlington Ridge.

The evolution of most names is traced, but the real name origin for "Nash" remains elusive. The best that can be concluded is: 1) it was borrowed from North Arlington, and, 2) there is no person of fame that relates to it – still a mystery!

Date written: 4/6/15 revised 4/10/15 revised 10/21/16 revised 12/30/2019
Printed with edit/modification in: The Arlington Historical Magazine, Vol 15 No 3, 2015 page 34

Before There Was a Pentagon

The Pentagon has been an Arlington landmark and monument to the US Defense establishment for nearly 80 years.

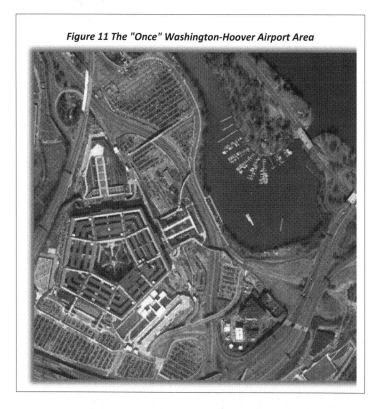

Figure 11 The "Once" Washington-Hoover Airport Area

Almost daily Charley and I walk to the end of Arlington Ridge Road to the high ground that was once Prospect Hill and the Civil War Fort Albany and can get a bird's eye view of all the Pentagon property – a grand building surrounded by acres of parking lots, heliport, 9/11 Pentagon Memorial park and Arlington Cemetery (Figure 11)[14].

Arlington Ridge Road once continued past its current northern terminus at Fort Albany through the heart of the area as it led to Arlington House (Lee Mansion).

It is hard to realize that for the hundred years before World War II the Pentagon area was a swamp, then farmland and part of the Arlington House (Lee Mansion) estate, then a location for a freed- slaves "Freedman's Village", and by the 1920's had a government experimental farm, a beach and amusement park, an equestrian racetrack, and two airports.

Freedman's Village consisted of fifty, two-family, two-story houses and was established by the federal government in 1863. The village's grounds included an industrial school, several schools for children, a hospital, a home for the aged and churches.

The Arlington Experimental Farm, "Arlington Farm", began in 1900 as a Department of Agriculture (USDA) crop research facility to develop new varieties of plants for American farmers. And then, there was a 38-acre Arlington County equestrian racetrack and the "Arlington Beach" amusement park that survived only a few years, in succession, were sold and demolished in 1929 to make way for the two airports.

While none of these property evolutions left a tangible legacy, perhaps the most interesting was the contribution of the two airports -- Hoover Field and Washington Airport. In the beginning they were separate and distinct businesses, then merged, then disappeared altogether. This is part of the story and excitement for commercial aviation -- and all the fits-and-starts of its beginnings.

In 1926 Hoover Field was named in honor of then Secretary of Commerce Herbert Hoover. The location and layout of Hoover Field, first owned by Potomac Flying Service, was described as "...a 2,000' x 800' rectangular sod field, with buildings on the southeast corner – including a roller coaster and amusement park."[15]

A second airport, Washington Airport, separated from Hoover Field by Military Road to the south, was owned by Seaboard Airlines. It had a small fleet of 8-passenger planes and began service in 1927. It was a triangular shaped sod 97-acre field, adjacent to Arlington Beach, an amusement park that was between the Potomac River and the airfield. Figure 12[16], a composite of vintage map sketches, successively "zooms in" (left-to-right) into the airports' locations.

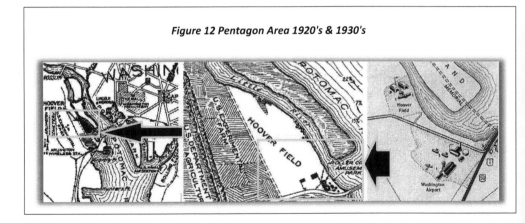

Figure 12 Pentagon Area 1920's & 1930's

The airfields ran passenger service, postal mail, and tourist flights over Washington. The Great Depression forced the owners of both Hoover and Washington Airports to sell to the National Aviation Corporation. The new owner merged the two fields, renamed the Washington-Hoover Airport, and built an art-deco terminal building, hangar, and outdoor swimming pool in 1930.

Washington-Hoover had a reputation as "...the poorest aviation ground facilities of any important city in the United States or Europe." Wiley Post remarked that "...there were better landing grounds in the wilds of Siberia than at Washington."

Flight operations were plagued by high-tension electrical wires, a high smokestack on one approach, a nearby burning garbage dump, and a single runway was intersected by the busy Military Road – that required guards to flag down traffic during takeoffs and landings. Compounding all the operational issues were site issues that precluded expansion since the site was bordered on the west by a railroad and on the east by Route 1 and the Potomac River. A combination of the river high water, a low-lying airport site, and poor drainage made the area subject to flooding. By 1941, with World War II looming and the need to build the Pentagon, and with Washington-Hoover's geographic liabilities, it was closed and replaced by the much larger Washington National Airport, two miles southeast (figure 13) [17]. A 1935, north-looking, aerial photograph (Figure 14)[18] shows Washington Airport in foreground and Hoover Field in background.

Figure 13 Washington Airport and 14th Street Bridge (mid-1920's)

Figure 14 Washington Airport (mid-1930's)

The Pentagon is a building built to last. Its location was a compromise of many site locations. But it stands on the shoulders of very interesting history – a history of evolving from swamp to farmland to a freed-slaves village to amusement parks and racetrack to the beginnings of America's commercial aviation history.

If you venture to Fort Albany Park, you too, like Charley and me can easily view the area and imagine the history from this overlook.

Date written: 10/27/18 revises 1/2/20

When Charley and I walk each day around Arlington Ridge, I often try to visualize what "The Ridge" looked like during and after the Civil War. If asked today what it looked like then, most people would likely say it was a forest-covered hill with a few stately mansions such as Prospect Hill and Green Valley Manor. The huge oaks and the upscale homes on Arlington Ridge Road that distinguish the area today must have been there for several hundred years – not so. The mansions no longer exist and parts of the terrain has been substantially reshaped eliminating ravines and other distinctive features (figure 15)[19].

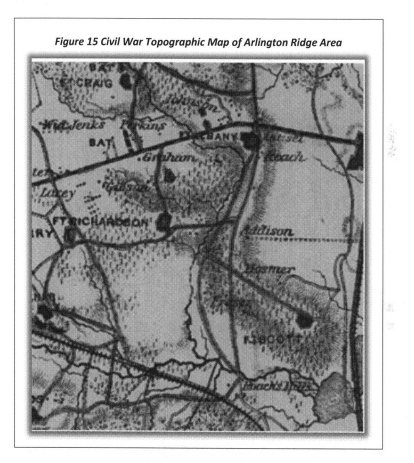

Figure 15 Civil War Topographic Map of Arlington Ridge Area

The Ridge can be generally defined as the L-shaped, high terrain between what was Fort Albany on the north and Fort Scott on the southeast leg of the L. At the outset of the war fort locations, located on confiscated, private lands owned by Roach, Fraser, Addison, and Hosmer, were selected at high points where they overlooked major routes of access into the City of Washington. Two forts on The Ridge were Fort Scott (now Fort

Scott Park) and Fort Albany (now part of Prospect Hill), that were supplemented by miles of rifle pits and connecting roads in between.

A picture taken from Arlington Ridge looking west, likely taken near the Addison house, shows the fort, on the right horizon, built in the fall of 1861. The dirt road leading up the hill toward the fort traces a route near the current Memorial Drive, a westerly extension of Addison Avenue, now South 20th Street (figure 16) [20]. The area also included tent camps and hospitals and a scattering of frame dwellings. In the fall of 1862, the new Convalescent Camp (Camp Metcalf) was built (replacing the camp near Alexandria) shown on the left horizon (Figure 16).

Nearly all the land was scalped of trees and low vegetation to build forts, supply firewood, and clear fields of fire and remained so to the war's end.

Figure 16 Fort Richardson as Viewed from Arlington Ridge

A picture (figure 17) [21] of Fort Richardson with its tent camp shows the view to the southeast with a hill area in the left distance --the Ridge.

While no two forts were alike their designs were relatively standard. A plan view of Fort Scott with today's streets and homes is a good simple portrayal of this design (figure 18). [22]

Figure 17 Arlington Ridge and Alexandria Viewed from Fort Richardson

Figure 18 Fort Scott Overlay with 1965 Dwellings

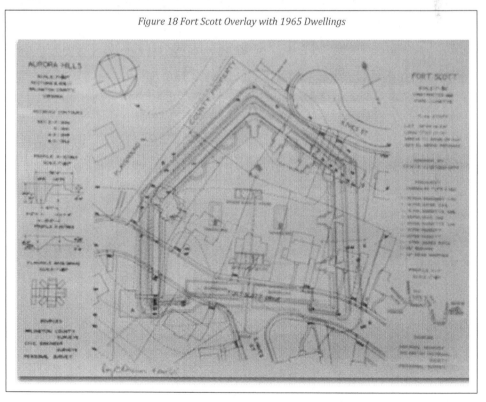

Interior bunkers were of timber with more than 10 feet of compacted earth to protect the magazines (ammunition and gunpowder) and the soldiers who manned the cannon which were the principle weapons. Buildings were of wood with metal roofs. Soldiers were housed in tent camps outside the earthworks.

Every fort had a well and a flag pole. The surrounding earthwork fortification would be of 12-18 foot high and fronted by a dry moat and sharpened poles embedded in the soil pointed in the direction of expected enemy advance.

The area of Fort Albany on Prospect Hill (note the Roach mansion to the right of picture) looks very different today – the excavation for the Interstate Highway cuts through most of the hill in the picture (figure 19)[23].

Figure 19 Fort Albany Looking North

Pencil sketches of The Ridge by Civil War soldiers show it as a barren, rounded hill. The large oaks of today that cover The Ridge didn't exist at the end of the War.

At the conclusion of the Civil War, on May 23-24, 1865, a two-day "Grand Review of the Armies" was held in Washington, D.C. The Army of the Potomac procession, May 23, was seven miles long. The Army of the Tennessee, Army of Georgia parade, May 24, was comprised of 65,000 soldiers. It is estimated the total number of soldiers in the parade numbered around 150,000. Mustering-out (armies disbanded and soldiers sent home) commenced once the parade ended, but the deactivation went on for months. For many Union soldiers, the last official campsite of the Civil War was on The Ridge.[24]

The numbers of men, horses, and equipment bivouacked on Arlington Ridge is hard to imagine. Parade formations covered an area of 7 miles by a width of a wide boulevard – about 200 acres – for two days. An encampment of tents to house the soldiers would likely require twice that space, not to mention all the logistic support – water, food, animal feed.

I'm convinced my second great grandfather, William A. Harper, after experiencing all four years of the war, ended his military career and his life on the Ridge. His grave is located in Arlington National Cemetery within a mile of the north end of the Ridge.

Men of Company K, at Fort C.F. Smith, north of The Ridge near the Potomac River, are frozen in time in a picture taken August 1865, after the war ended (figure 20)[25]. William A. Harper, Company K, 2d New York Heavy Artillery was stationed at both Forts C.F. Smith and Albany and may be in that picture.

Figure 20 Company K, 2d New York Heavy Artillery, Fort C.F. Smith

The story of his Civil War journey is highlighted in the following table that identifies existing letters from him and his unit locations of the 2d New York Heavy Artillery. He died in Douglas Hospital in Washington, DC of dystentery 5 months after the war was over (figure 21).

Figure 21 William A. Harper Civil War Chronology

July 21, 1861 First Battle of Bull Run, Virginia
September 27, 1861, letter from WAH, Ox Run (Bull Run, Virginia)
September 8, 1862, 2d New York Heavy Artillery mustered in.
July 13-18, 1863 WAH enlisted and mustered in – official records (no mention of earlier service documented in 1861 letter)
October 2, 1864, letter from WAH, Fortress Monroe, Virginia
January 14, 1965, letter from WAH, Carolina City, North Carolina
April 7, 1865, letter from WAH, Goldsboro, North Carolina
April 9, 1865.Civil War ended
May 23-24, 1865 parade in Washington, District of Columbia
May 27, 1865, letter from WAH, Greensboro, North Carolina
June 27, 1865 2d New York Heavy Artillery consolidated into 4 companies.
July 6, 1865 2d New York Heavy Artillery mustered out at Washington, District of Columbia; soldiers not eligible transferred to 2d New York Volunteer Artillery (companies I, J, K, L) – stationed at Fort Albany and Fort C.F. Smith
September 29, 1865, WAH mustered out of Union Army, Company K, 2d New York Heavy Artillery,
October 4, 1865 WAH admitted to Douglas Hospital, Washington, District of Columbia
October 21, 1865, WAH died leaving a 25-year old wife with 5 children under the age of 9.

The last unit to occupy Fort Albany was the 2d New York Heavy Artillery.

As Charley and I walked the Ridge this winter morning, particularly over the area of Fort Albany, I sense we are walking atop Corporal Harper's last encampment.

Date written: 1/11/2016 revised 12/30/2019

Founding Families of Arlington Ridge: Prospect Hill

Sometimes I feel as though Charley and I, on our twice a day walks; cover every street, every day on Arlington Ridge. But that's not reasonable, since there are about 20 miles of streets and alleys on the Ridge and we only do 6 to 8 miles per day.

A couple times each week, however, Charley and I walk to Prospect Hill, an overlook of the Pentagon on a finger of land formerly known as Hoe Hill (or "Nob Hill") at the highest most northern site on the ridge(figure 22)[26] .

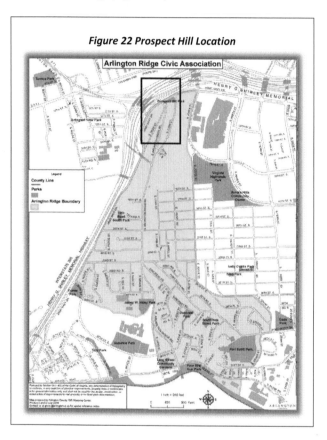

Figure 22 Prospect Hill Location

The land was part of the original 1669 patent of Captain Robert Howson, then purchased by John Alexander and passed to son Phillip, then conveyed to William Henry Washington in 1811, then taken over by the Bank of the United States in 1835, and purchased by James Roach in 1837.

Construction of the Prospect Hill manor, by James Roach, was started in 1840 and completed the next year. It was still part of the Capitol City District until retrocession to Virginia in 1846.

Figure 23 Prospect Hill Manor

Prospect Hill Manor (figure 23) [27] held a commanding view of the Arlington Mansion and Cemetery, Potomac River, Capitol Building, Washington Monument, and White House. At the outset of the Civil War the house was occupied by Union soldiers, Forts Albany and Runyon were built on the property, and the Roaches were imprisoned until the war ended. The property was sold in 1869 to settle claims against the estate and broken up into lots of 20-60 acres.

The mansion fell into ruin. Rescued in 1913 by Philip and Helen Campbell (Phillip was a Congressman from Kansas), the mansion was restored. Upon the death of Helen Campbell in the 1960's, all four heirs had no interest in occupying the property and entered into an agreement for rezoning – it is now The Representative high-rise condominium – home to many notables.

A column, "With The Rambler", that appeared in the Washington Evening Star in 1915 there appeared a good description of Prospect Hill and the remains of Fort Albany in that year. Excerpted from the article is the following description:

"Crossing the Columbia Pike and climbing the grade beyond, you come to a height where, weedy and tangle grown, rest the ruins of Fort Albany, and in these, ruins stands a brick church about which the Rambler has previously written and which, from most of the high points in Washington and its northern and eastern environs, is a sky mark on the Virginia hills. It is Mount Zion Colored Baptist Church. It is a bold brick structure, with red sides, a dun front and was erected in 1884. The congregation was organized by ex-slaves, either just before or after emancipation and that congregation worshiped in a small frame building in the nearby settlement of Freedmen's City, or as it was often called, Freedmen's village. That was the village which was wiped out by the southeastly extension of the Arlington grounds...

A few hundred yards ahead of you and on the east crest of the ridge, rising out of a lacework of trees just touched with the promise of green leaf buds, you see two tall square chimneys, heavy red brick walls, white pillared porches and bright green shutters. It is a noble old house, and you note that some new owner has taken it under his charge. It is sprucing up and telling every passerby that good times have come. For years the Rambler has known that old house. For years it has spoken of its neglect to everybody who passed that way. The fine gardens, that in happier days bloomed around it, were ruinous and dejected, but the old house, even when it hungered for fresh paint and stood in dire need of window glass and blinds, always looked proudly, almost defiantly, out upon the road. But the house seems very happy now. Prosperity gives it a cheerful tone. The grounds have been cleared up, a jungle of shiftless growth has been cleared away and a gardener was setting out in fresh, new beds scores of ornamental shrubs when the Rambler walked that way. Long before the civil war that house was the home of Jacob Roach, a considerable landholder thereabouts. He owned a grist mill on Four Mile run, and on the old maps you can mark the exact location of Roach's mill. As a contractor he made much money out of the building of the Loudoun and Hampshire railroad, which became the Bluemont division of the Southern railway and is now the electric line to Leesburg and Bluemont. The Rambler has been told that James Roach at the outbreak of the civil war organized a cavalry troop, entered the Confederate army and did not return to his home overlooking Washington. The place came into possession of a nephew, who was a bachelor, and finally fell into the hands of others than members of the Roach family. The Rambler has striven to find out more about the Roach family and the owners of this land, before James Roach came to live there, but his efforts have as yet yielded no fruit. It is said that the land records of that part of the country were destroyed during the civil war."

The two Sanborn Fire Insurance map pictures, before and after 1940, (figures 24 & 25)[28] clearly show the Campbell properties, to the east of the sharp left turn as northbound Arlington Ridge Road becomes southbound South Nash Street.

Figure 24 Sanborn Fire Insurance Map of Campbell Property -- before 1940	Figure 25 Sanborn Fire Insurance Map of Campbell Property -- after 1940

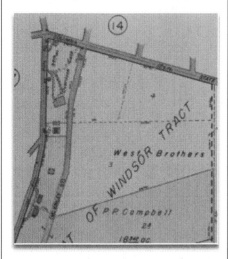 

When the Pentagon was attacked on 9/11/2001, I could walk down Arlington Ridge Road to Prospect Hill and watch the fire and smoke billowing from the building.

Every day, when Charley and I pass that overlook point, I relive that moment and the great history viewed from that lofty perch – and Charley enjoys the view and sniffing the grass.

Date written: 6/30/15 revised 12/30/2019

A couple of times a week Charley and I walk half of the perimeter of Arlington Ridge varying the trip by covering the west side one day, then the east side the next. As we come around the northernmost end near the Pentagon we pass by large vertical concrete walls of Prospect Hill that over 150 years ago would have been under the Civil War-era Fort Albany and near what was once the Federal-style mansion built by the Roach family.

That part of the Ridge had the evolving names of "Hoes Hill", "Prospect Hill" in the 1800's , and "Sunnyside" in the 1900's.

The story of the location's evolution from plantation, to war, to renaissance, to demolition is well documented in the Arlington Historical Society Journal article, "Prospect Hill".[29]

Standing today near the Air Force Memorial, oriented south, and attempting to imagine "Fort Albany of Arlington Heights" from the 1861 perspective, you would now be facing the 25-foot high concrete retaining walls of the cutaway Arlington Ridge – now imagine Fort Scott and the Prospect Hill mansion . The mansion would be the structure in the distance at the left of the drawing – replaced by The Representative, a sprawling and towering condominium (figure 26)[30].

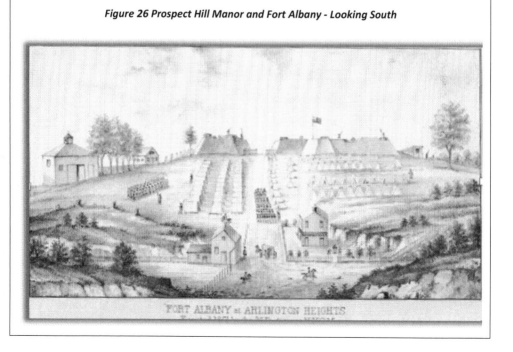

Figure 26 Prospect Hill Manor and Fort Albany - Looking South

FORT ALBANY at ARLINGTON HEIGHTS

Recently I met with a long time Arlington Ridge resident, Ann Donohough. She not only has lived on the Ridge her whole life, but was a student at the historic Hume School. As we discussed various interesting tales of the Ridge focusing on very old residences, she kept coming back to the "mess" that was created by the cut through the Prospect Hill property at the time of the building of the Pentagon in 1941. She remembered the seemingly endless period characterized by mud, confusion, and traffic snarls. The latter mess was caused by the new clover-leaf circles that seemed difficult for drivers to master (figures 27 & 28) [31].

When this story was started I had intended that Roach's Prospect Hill house would be the focus, but quickly realized there was larger story that included what was called the "mixing bowl" project.

The "mixing bowl" involved moving an estimated 1.5 million cubic yards of earth – the volume of the Great Pyramid at Giza is double that amount, but is a manmade wonder of the world. The project also involved 68 thousand cubic yards of concrete emplacement with 9 thousand tons of structural and reinforcing steel and 13.6 miles of underdrains. Before and after aerial images centered on wooded area and Prospect Hill mansion clearly portray the enormity of the effort.

The mansion would later be demolished in 1965 to provide the site for The Representative luxury condominium high rise structure. Coupled with the "mixing bowl" project, a page of Arlington history was more than turned, it was obliterated.

The physical remains of the first hundred years of history are gone except for a historic placard marker, but Prospect Hill is still a beautiful place to walk on a nice Spring day and view the Pentagon, Arlington Cemetery, and Washington. A good place for man and dog to stop and take a break before heading back home.

Figure 27 "Mixing Bowl" Under Construction

Figure 28 "Mixing Bowl" Completed

Date written: 5/31/2016 revised 1/4/2020

Walking around the Ridge residents can take pride in most of what has replaced many of the down-slope parts that were industrial and run down. On our walks Charley and I greet smiling neighbors, dogs, modern buildings, and wonderful scenic views. In particular, as we traverse the pointed end of the Ridge up toward the Pentagon, there are the following beautiful high-rise buildings (figure 29).

Figure 29 Arlington Ridge High-Rise Buildings

The Representative (1101 South Arlington Ridge Road, 1976, condominium, units:206) on Prospect Hill/Sunnyside
The Cavendish (1200 & 1300 South Arlington Ridge Road, 1958/1981, condominium, units:198)
Ridge House (1301 South Arlington Ridge Rd, 1964/1979, condominium, units: 89) on The Little Tea House
Pentagon Ridge (1515 South Arlington Ridge Road, 1974, condominium, units: 32)
Parliament House (1512 S Arlington Ridge Road, 1964, apartments, units: 33)

Some buildings that started out as apartments (e.g, The Cavendish, Pentagon Ridge, Ridge House) were then converted to condominium, The Representative was condominium from the beginning, and Parliament House is mixed apartment/condominium.

Previous stories in this book (Fort Albany, Prospect Hill/Sunnyside) relate the historical evolution of the land that is now The Representative. Little remains of the earlier structures that preceded these current buildings, except historic placards about Fort Albany and Prospect Hill and "The Wellhouse" (figure 30) [32].

Figure 30 Little Tea House Wellhouse

The Little Tea House owned (figure 31) [33] and managed by Gertrude Crocker starting in 1920 is one a few locations on Arlington Ridge that people know about, but usually can't recall much detail.

The small, circular stone building that was once part of the Little Tea House restaurant, near the intersection of South Lynn Street and Arlington Ridge Road, is the "The Wellhouse", now used for pool maintenance for The Ridge Condominiums (figure 32) [34].

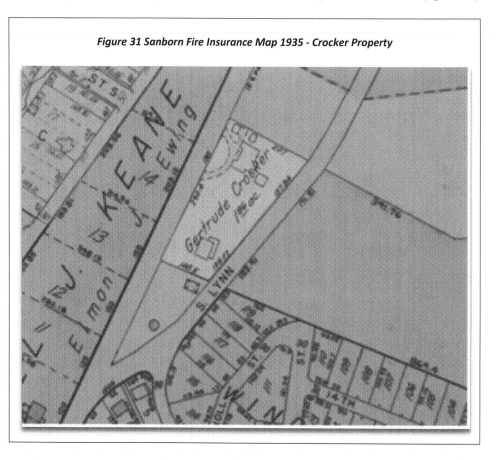

Figure 31 Sanborn Fire Insurance Map 1935 - Crocker Property

According to noted Arlington historian Eleanor Lee Templeton,
  "...probably more important world decisions were consummated over the tables of The Little Tea House than in Washington. Over the years, one would find Mrs. Eleanor Roosevelt and Mrs. Morgenthau at lunch; Mrs. Harding entertaining cabinet wives at tea; Chief Justice Oliver Wendall Holmes enjoying dinner. Amelia Earhart would come directly up from Hoover Airport (the present site of the Pentagon Lagoon), to discuss plans for an improved and enlarged National Airport."

Figure 32 The Ridge Condominium and Wellhouse

An advertisement in a 1936 magazine (figure 33) [35] featured the automatic coal burner oven "Iron Fireman that cooks food, heats water, and warms the famous Little Tea House." The ad says: "Of the many fine places to eat in Washington, D.C. area is the Little Tea House. If you know Washington, you know this picturesque retreat on Arlington Ridge, which commands a magnificent vista over the Potomac River and the city." The caption to the picture of the house in the same advertisement includes the following: "Here the wives of four Presidents have come to enjoy the beauty and its [Tea House] special dishes."

Figure 33 Magazine Advertisement (Little Tea House)

ALEXANDRIA VA 1936

GERTRUDE LYNDE CROCKER
discovers and adopts
IRON FIREMAN COAL FIRING

IRON FIREMAN *cooks food, heats water and warms the famous Little Tea House*

OF THE many fine places to eat in Washington, D. C., one of the most charming is the Little Tea House. If you know Washington, you know this picturesque retreat on Arlington Ridge, which commands a magnificent vista over the Potomac River and the city.

What you may not know is that the cheerful warmth of the Little Tea House is provided by an Iron Fireman automatic coal burner. The delicious food is cooked on a modern coal range which is fired by an Iron Fireman coal burner.

Miss Gertrude L. Crocker, owner and manager, whose success has been built around the word *quality*, is generous in her praise. She does not exaggerate when she says, "Iron Fireman equipment is the best investment I have made in a long time." Her statement is based upon the fact that Iron Fireman, replacing oil and gas, cut the cost of heating and hot water from $630 to $200 in one season.

Having saved 2/3 of every heating dollar, Miss Crocker replaced her gas cooking range with a coal range equipped with Iron Fireman. Once again Iron Fireman cut fuel bills 2/3, and Miss Crocker says, "This range is quiet, clean, simple and easy to operate, economical and most efficient. I expect that Iron Fireman will pay for itself in one year in fuel savings alone."

What Iron Fireman has done for Miss Crocker it should be able to do for you in your business and in your home. An installation can be made quickly in old or new residential heating plants and in commercial or industrial boilers developing up to 500 h.p. Convenient monthly payment terms. If you want better heat or power plus substantial fuel savings, ask your Iron Fireman dealer for a free survey, or write to 3024 W. 106th St., Cleveland for literature. Iron Fireman Mfg. Co., Portland, Oregon; Cleveland; Toronto. Dealers everywhere.

IRON FIREMAN
AUTOMATIC COAL BURNER

· 195 ·

The 1920's menu (figures 34 & 35) indicates "Served from 12 – 830 P.M." and had a four course Tenderloin Steak dinner including "Hot Bread and Beverages" for $1.50.

Figure 34 Little Tea House Menu Cover

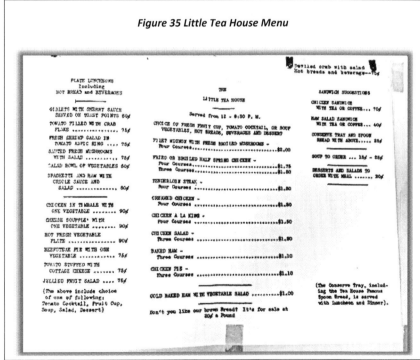

Figure 35 Little Tea House Menu

Gertrude Lynde Crocker leased and later sold the business to Gertrude Allison. For a short while it became known as Allison's Little Tea House.

Gertrude was an early student in Julia Child's L'Ecole des Gourmettes cooking school in Paris. In Child's book, My Life in France, she commented:

> "Gertrude Allison had spent three years in the cafeteria business, had studied home economics at Columbia University, and had a sound business sense. She ran an inn in Arlington, Virginia, called Allison's Little Tea House, which catered mostly to officers from the Pentagon at lunchtime and to family groups in the evening. Gertrude said she had taken several cooking classes in New York with the English chef Dione Lucas, whom she found adept but not very precise. I quizzed Gertrude about the economics of her restaurant. She charged $1.75 to $3.50 for dinner, she said, adding that studies showed that restaurateurs shouldn't pay more than 6 percent of their gross for rent."[36]

The Little Tea House (figures 36 & 37)[37] was demolished in 1963 to allow construction of The Ridge apartment building, later converted to condominium.

Figure 36 Little Tea House Interior

Figure 37 Little Tea House Entrance

The other high-rise buildings (The Cavendish, Pentagon Ridge, and Parliament House) were constructed on areas that were largely pasture, or undeveloped, hillside landscape that holds little historical significance.

Pentagon Ridge, however, does have a twentieth century story. In 1974, East Germany built Pentagon Ridge to house its staff members as an apartment – less than half a mile from the Pentagon, two miles from the White House and Capitol – in clear sight!

After disintegration of the Soviet Union and with German reunification, the building was sold and turned into condominium.

Date written: 10/4/2016 revised 5/19/2017 revised 1/2/2020

Long-Gone WWII Ridge Housing

As Charley and I walk the large parking lots east of the Ridge between The River House high-rise buildings (between Arlington Ridge Road and South Lynn Street), we try to envision what the JEB Stuart homes might have looked like during and after WWII.

Defense Homes Corporation built homes to house the rapid expanding Pentagon workforce. The JEB Stuart and Jubal Early homes were erected to standards not in accordance with Arlington County building code, and thus, were demolished after the war.

There are no streets. foundations, nor historic placards of those developments today.

As Charley and I walk further toward Crystal City we try to look for any trace of the JEB Stuart Homes in the area of the River House condominiums (Top-center rectangle #1 in figure 38) and Jubal Early Homes that were between South Fern Street and Jeff Davis Highway and 18th and 23rd Streets (Center-right rectangle #2 in figure 38) [38].

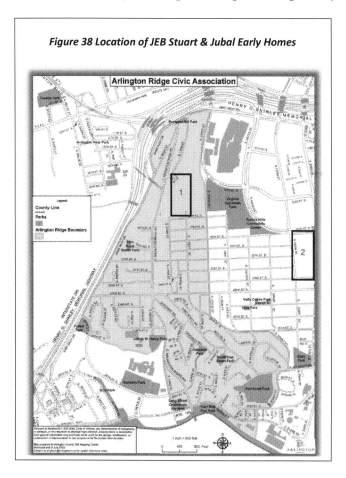

Figure 38 Location of JEB Stuart & Jubal Early Homes

The black circle on the accompanying Sanborn Fire Insurance map below identifies the area of the WWII-era JEB Stuart homes picture (figure 39) [39] [40]. While they were still multi-story blocks of homes, their design was different from the Jubal Early homes.

Figure 39 JEB Stuart Homes – 1947 Sanborn Fire Insurance Map & Picture

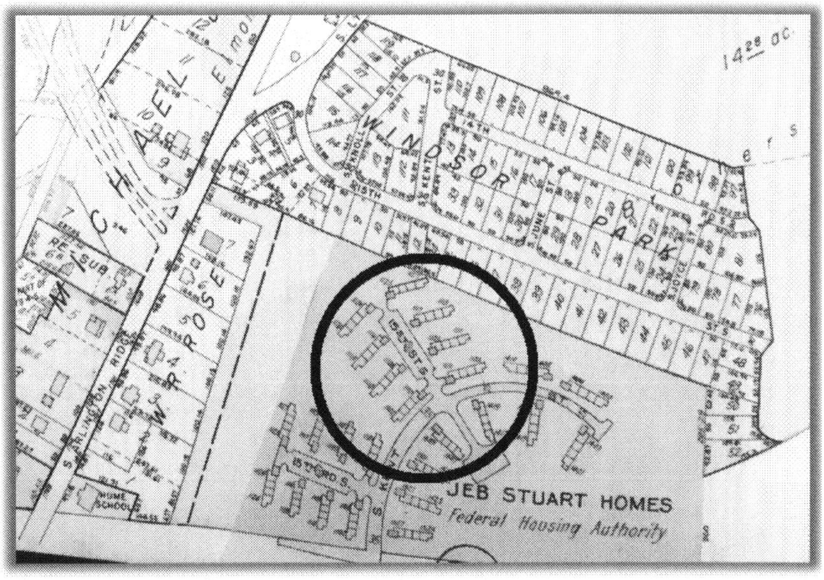

The row of Jubal Early houses in the picture below is noted (black oval west of S. Eads Street and between S. 22 rd and S. 23rd Streets) and on the accompanying Sanborn Fire Insurance map. The area looked like many other WWII-era, temporary, offices and houses on military installations and continued to exist well into the 1970's.
In Arlington, only pictures and a few memories remain (figure 40) [41] [42].

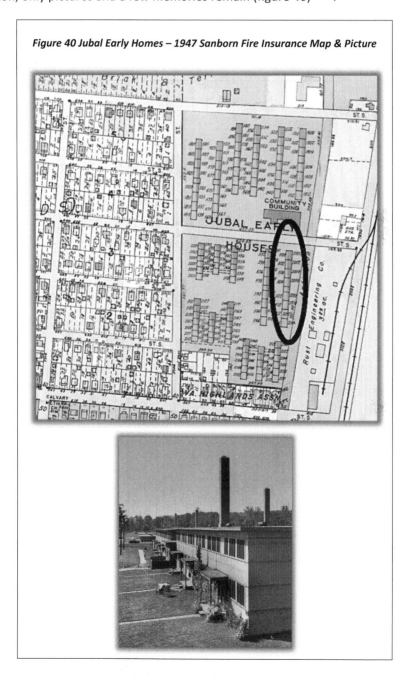

Figure 40 Jubal Early Homes – 1947 Sanborn Fire Insurance Map & Picture

Two women, writing in an Arlington Central Library blog in 2013[43], remember:

"I remember living with my grandmother on Twentieth Street in Arlington during WWII when my father was in Europe. We were not allowed to go near the housing project that, until I was an adult, I always thought was called Jubalalie. "

"Our family lived there I believe in the mid to late forties. We were very close to all of the other families and it was safe and fun. I can remember snips of the way the house looked (I was about 5 when we moved). My older brother and I shared one of the two bedrooms – I remember it was barely big enough for the bunk beds and 2 dressers; a small living/dining area adjacent to a small open kitchen. Even though it was small and considered low income housing, my memories are of love and family."

Date written: 10/4/2016 revised 1/2/2020

Often Charley and I often walk the north-end of Arlington Ridge then down to Eads Street. Today the area is well-developed with modern high-rise buildings that include Pentagon City and Crystal City.

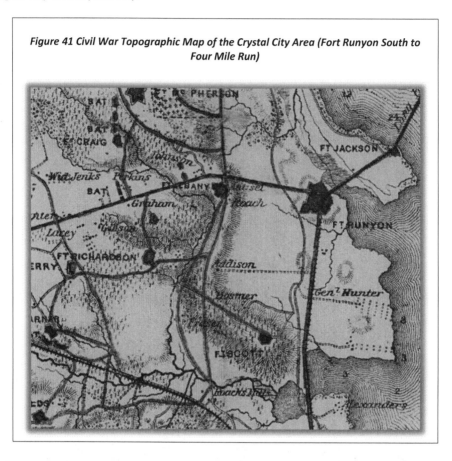

Figure 41 Civil War Topographic Map of the Crystal City Area (Fort Runyon South to Four Mile Run)

Crystal City wasn't always an area of modern office towers and transit lines. The area before the 1900's included, two Civil War forts, Albany and Runyon, and "Jackson City" (so named in 1835, after President Andrew Jackson) that housed a racetrack and was a Washington outpost near what is now Boundary Channel Drive (figure 41)[44]. After the war ended, the area deteriorated into a collection of brothels, betting parlors, and saloons, much like Rosslyn during the same period. In 1904 a self-appointed vigilante cleanup crew known as the "Good Citizens League", burned most of the buildings. From those ashes, the area became an industrial sprawl of brickyards, warehouses, iron-fabricating factories, rail yards and junkyards.

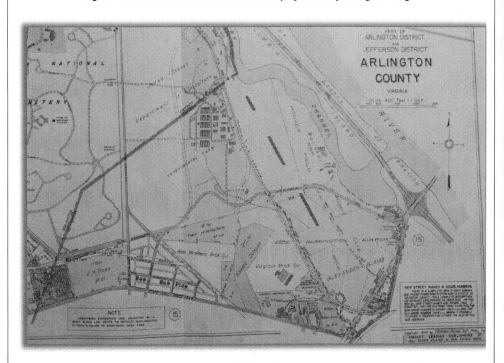

Figure 42 1935 Sanborn Fire Insurance Map of North of Arlington Ridge

Before there was a Pentagon the majority of the "Jackson City" land was dedicated to an Experimental Farm, airports, and 10 brick plants using local clays to produce red brick for sale in Washington (Lower Right Quadrant of Map, figure 42) [45].

The location was ideal for that type of business due to the proximity of large clay deposits along the shoreline of the nearby Potomac River. One of the largest plants was West Brothers Brick Company (figure 43) [46]. Founded shortly after the Civil War, it remained in operation until the land was taken over by the federal government in 1942 to build the Pentagon. Destroyed by fire in 1939, brick making ceased, but the property became land for WWII area leasing opportunities including the WWII housing (Jubal Early Homes), an Airport Drive-In Movie Theater (1947-1963) at the intersection of Jefferson Davis Highway and South 20th Street (figure 44) [47], a Safeway store, and a bowling alley.

Figure 43 West Brothers Brick Company

Figure 44 Airport Drive-in Movie Theater

However, the real transformation began in 1964 with the building of the Crystal House apartments on leased land of The Brick Companies, successor to the West Brothers Brick Company. Crystal House was so named because of the large crystal chandelier hung in the lobby -- removed when the apartments were converted to condominium. During the 1960's an additional six office buildings and two more apartment buildings along with underground retail space and parking, known as Crystal Plaza, Crystal Towers and the Marriott Crystal Gateway Hotel becoming known as Crystal City.

The transformation from brick manufacturing to property leasing with Crystal City, then to property development, is an interesting tale of the evolution of the various brick manufacturing companies that have now morphed into a company call "The Brick Companies." The company, now based in Edgewater, Maryland, owns, develops and manages commercial, residential and recreational properties in and around the District of Columbia, Maryland, and Virginia – a far cry from the ashes of the seedy Jackson City.

Date written: 8/29/2016 revised 1/2/2020

Arlington Ridge Mysteries: Summer Cottages and Trolleys

If you walk every street and alley—just one way--in Arlington Ridge you will travel approximately 20 miles. Regardless, of how long and how much you walk, The Ridge is an area that keeps unveiling something new not seen before. I've been walking the area for nearly twenty-five years and discover something new every day. There are also the unseen or unknown layers of history that, when exposed, reveal even more myths, unknowns, and mysteries.

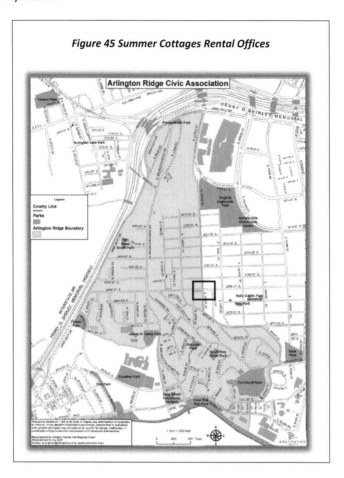

Figure 45 Summer Cottages Rental Offices

One of the myths of the Ridge is that the houses at the intersection of Arlington Ridge Road and South 23rd Street (figure 45) are the last of the summer cottages that used to populate the area (figure 46) [48].

In fact, the small buildings that remain near the intersection with South 23rd Street were originally zoned "commercial" and served as the rental offices for the larger summer homes on the Ridge. The building with "Neighborhood Realty" signage today is the single remaining "commercial" building. It is a one-room office with a small corner restroom. The cottage, at times, has housed up to six agents in an area that might be comfortable for one. One building was expanded to become much larger family home and the other survives as a very small residence. All remaining and former old houses along the Ridge all have a story.

Figure 46 Summer Cottages Realty Office

Currently, buildings along Arlington Ridge Road include a mix of new and old houses some dating to the 1930-40s. At an elevation 150 feet above the Potomac River older residences were built as vacation homes taking advantage of the breezes and overlooking the Potomac River. Unfortunately, many of the wonderful vintage homes are being replaced by "McMansions."

Another myth about Ridge is that a trolley line once ran directly alongside Arlington Ridge Road. According to a Wikipedia page on Arlington Ridge Road, "Washington, Alexandria, and Mount Vernon Railway, a streetcar company, built its East Arlington branch to Arlington National Cemetery in 1895. Along most of its route, this branch of the streetcar railway traveled parallel to and just east of Arlington Ridge Road ".[49] This article would lead readers to believe there was a trolley line along the Ridge very near Arlington Ridge Road. It was actually a mile down the slope between S. Eads Street and Richmond Highway.

By 1910, Arlington Ridge had commuter trolley access to Washington DC, with four stops along Jefferson Avenue (now Eads Street): Four Mile Run, the Car Barn, 22nd

Street, and 18th Street (figure 47)[50]. From any of these stops it would have been a significant uphill hike to the Ridge. Later bus transportation beat out trolley transportation and the last trolley rolled down the area in early 1932. No tracks remain, and the last vestiges were recently removed with residential construction in the 800 block of South 21st Street.

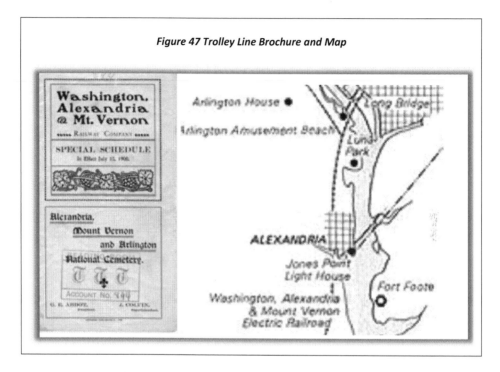

Figure 47 Trolley Line Brochure and Map

Until the 1980's Arlington Ridge Road was a heavily traveled divided roadway with median strip, despite its largely residential character. The road was modified by eliminating the median, which allowed for the creation of sidewalks and grass service strips between the sidewalks and roadway. However, today, when it is rush hour and southbound I-395 is a parking lot, Arlington Ridge Road and the "summer cottages" route becomes a new relief valve for those suffering to leave Washington, DC.

Date written: 6/2/15 revised 1/2/2020

Charley and I walk through Haley Park (figure 48, black square) at least once a day.
Haley Park is the point in our walk where she can go off her lead. Often her Golden
Retriever nose picks up the scent of the foxes that have several dens in the surrounding
woods and have been crossing the area during the night hours.

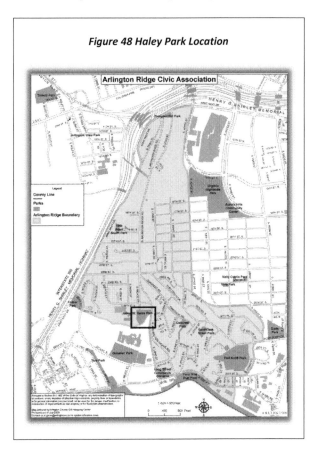

Figure 48 Haley Park Location

In 1890 a single-family frame dwelling with a garage was built on the site of 2400 South
Meade Street (figure 49)[51].

The Arlington County building card for the property owned by James W. Haley has a
record of Building Permit 8156, dated 2/7/52 "reroof dwelling", but then a handwritten
note was scrawled across the card: "Demolish and remove 2 story frame bldg. Garage to
stay -- Cty to remove 4/7/76 McLeod say garage is also down". When a house is
demolished the building history record is usually deleted. Arlington County condemned
the house and demolished it in 1976. The family agreed to a settlement ($190,000), as
long as the property would be named James W. Haley Park.

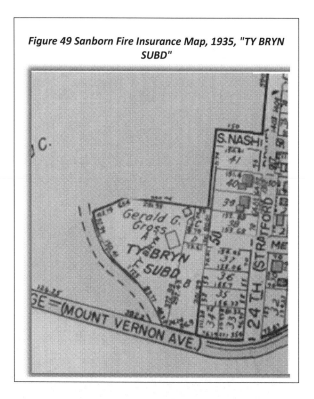

Figure 49 Sanborn Fire Insurance Map, 1935, "TY BRYN SUBD"

The owner of the house before the Haley's bought it in 1940 was Gerald Gross. A 1935 Sanborn Fire Insurance map (with updates to 1941) identifies the property of Gerald G. Gross with a Welsh nickname of Ty Bryn, "Hill House", in Gaelic (figure 49) [52].

Figure 50 Hill House, 1970

In interviews with retired judge James W. Haley, Jr., Judge Haley talked about growing up in Arlington, Virginia, and the influence of his parents. His father, James W. Haley, was a lawyer and Vice President/General Counsel for the National Coal Council; his mother was an attorney for the Treasury Department. He also related many interesting stories about the property and Arlington Ridge and contiguous areas.

Judge Haley grew up in the house and then moved in 1957 when his father bought a "grand" North Arlington house on N. 26th Street near Washington Golf and Country Club. The house was then rented to a Navy Captain Bell 1957-70. Judge Haley moved back to the house with his family 1970-1972 (figure 50) [53]. The house was then rented again 1972-1976. It fell into disrepair and was destroyed in 1976.

Fred Korth rented the house on the property to the east of the Haley's for many years. Korth was an Assistant Secretary of Army during the Truman Administration and became Secretary of the Navy during the Kennedy Administration.

Figure 51 Hill House (Looking Uphill) & Wisteria Bush

I talked with Judge Haley several times and developed the following picture of the house and neighborhood. Judge Haley remembers:

> "The area, now occupied by Oak Ridge Elementary School (built in the 1940's), was a large blackberry patch and the area now occupied by Gunston Middle School (built in the 1970's) was all small "slum" homes called "Shirley Homes". The current trail in the park area between the house and the middle school was an old road connection to Arlington Ridge Road. There was a concrete bridge (some abutment structures remain) over the streambed that was a haven for "bums". After the middle school was built, the residents had great difficulty keeping school children from climbing the hill and cutting through the property. The house was on a septic field and had its own well attached to a shed on the west side of the house. The property had a biologically unique Hawthorne tree and an enormous, greater than 25 feet tall Wisteria bush (see picture of children holding blossoms, figure 51) that bordered the property on the east side. Haley still has in his possession a fossil, verified by the Smithsonian, found on the property. The house, during the 1950's, was under the flight path into the National (now Reagan) Airport. One night an airplane, making an approach clipped the treetops on the property. The Haley family had a live-in, widowed maid, Mary Thompson Grant, who was a nanny for James as a child.   The house was originally heated by coal delivered by the Uline Company, a company that also underwrote the development of Uline Arena, later the Washington Coliseum. Alexandria Dairy delivered milk and "Holmes to Homes Bread Delivery" delivered bread."

Rumors among children when Judge Haley was growing up were that Gross was German-born and a German spy – they even found a short-wave radio parts "hidden" in the garage along with the WWII blackout curtains. The actual owner was Gerald C. Gross, who was a former naval officer and worked as a federal employee and was born in Brooklyn, New York.

Date written: 7/29/2015 revised 1/3/2020

One of Charley's and my favorite nighttime walks is to the large field behind Oakridge School. Like many Arlington schools the campus is posted with strict anti-dog warning signs (figure 52) [54].

Figure 52 "NO DOGS" - Not even Charley

We don't go there when school is in session nor when children are playing outside, but the large grassed area behind the school with its baseball diamond, basketball courts, and play structures is a large "dog playground". Charley and I are not the only neighbors who use it and don't heed the warnings. Regardless, we, and all that we associate with, are always responsible to ensure we pick up "after play".

Our time to go, nearly every night throughout the year, is after Final Jeopardy (8pm). In the summer it's still light at that hour and "chase the ball" is great exercise. In winter it is usually very dark, often very cold and our tracks in the snow or ice are a record of our solitary passage.

Built in 1950 on 8-1/4 acres of a strawberry field, Oakridge is on Arlington Ridge high ground above the Gunston area at 1414 South 24th Street. The school was originally going to be named Hume Elementary School, but the name was changed to Oakridge prior to its dedication on April 8, 1951 so as not to be confused with the historic Hume School (figure 53)[55] .

The Queen Anne-style Hume School building, built in 1891 and closed in 1958, about a mile from Oakridge, no longer has students and is a museum and offices of the Arlington Historical Society.

Figure 53 Hume School

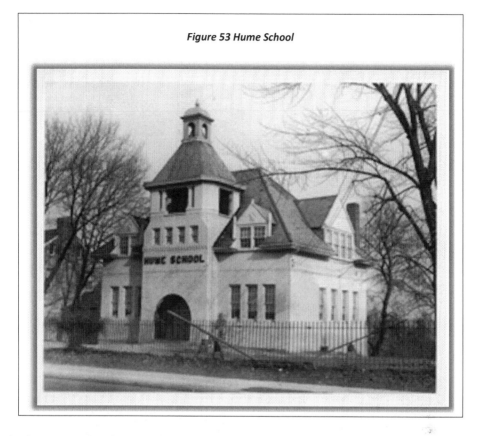

Oakridge opened in the Fall of 1950 prior to its completion. As reported in the March 9, 1951 edition of the Northern Virginina Sun, "Serious delays were caused by material shortages which arose after the Korean crisis...." The April 13, 1951 newspaper article led with "Theme of the opening ceremony at the new Oakridge School Sunday afternoon was "Oakridge as a Community Center".

A paved wilderness trail connecting Haley Park and Gunston Middle School exits the rear of the fenced Oakridge campus at its southwest corner and runs in an easterly direction along the backside of a densely wooded, steep-sloped protected area that contains many fox dens (figure 54)[56].

Figure 54 Charley - Evading "NO DOGS" Signs

The scent of fox and chasing the ball are sports for Charley's Golden Retriever nose and fitness.

Date written: 8/23/2016 revised 1/3/2020

Schools of the Ridge: Dolley Madison School

As opposed to the exciting and very memorable high school years, my experience of asking older adults what they remember about junior high/middle school is "not much". But there are yearbooks and reunions.

What happens when a school, particularly an elementary or junior high school, disappears? It is unlikely there were yearbooks and reunions.

But, for at least a generation or two there must be memories and stories. What about Dolley Madison Junior High School? It completely disappeared, but it did have a yearbook.

Many junior high schools, if they didn't disappear went through name changing in the late 1960's becoming middle schools. The grade levels of students that attended was likely 7-9, the early teenage years – chaotic hormonal physical and mental turmoil . The 1950's were the years of poodle skirts, greasers, atomic bomb drills, and segregation. Teens used typewriters, had phonographs to play records, and were able to go home or stay at school for lunch. Most schools had a library and most teens lived within walking distance of their school and friends.

The Dolley Madison Junior High School opened September 17, 1945 with 435 students, mostly from Arlington Ridge. The building façade was the cover for the 1948-1949 Yearbook (figure 55) [57].

Figure 55 Dolley Madison Junior High School Yearbook Cover

Students from the Ridge crossed under Shirley Highway through a underground tunnel to the school. That tunnel still exists, but is now closed with a barred, unlocked gate and sign saying "DANGER PROCEED AT YOUR OWN RISK".

By a mutual agreement, the the property of Dolley Madison School was transferred to Arlington County from Army Navy Country Club for $20. The original path for Army Navy Drive, bounded the school to the north and Shirley Highway bounded the property to southeast[58]. The construction of Shirley Highway and the Pentagon road system altered much of historic paths in the area to include Army Navy Drive and Long Branch Creek, so old boundaries can be confusing without good and old maps (figure 56) [59].

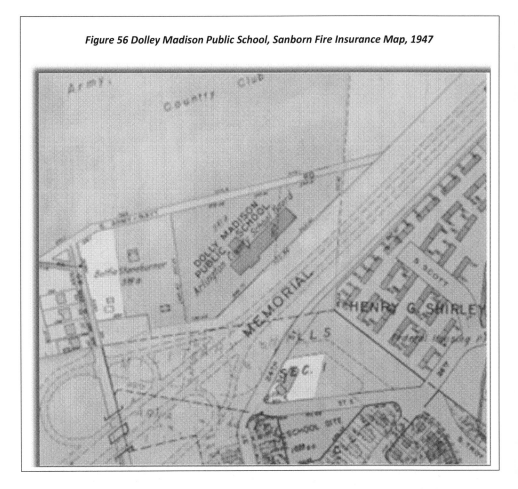

Figure 56 Dolley Madison Public School, Sanborn Fire Insurance Map, 1947

It served as a junior high school until the mid-1950s when it was replaced by Gunston Junior High (later Gunston Middle School).

In 1965 the property was sold to commercial developers, the school building demolished. But the name of first lady Dolley Madison lives on...in spirit ...and old year books (figure 57)[60].

Figure 57 Dolley Madison Towers

Date written: 8/23/2016 revised 1/3/2020

As Charley and I walk around a circuit of South 28th Street toward South Lang Street and Arlington Ridge Road, we see more signs indicating "No Dogs Allowed". I have to believe there is an exception for a Goldendoodle named Charley who started her "working career" as a therapy dog at Gunston Middle School as a guest of Animal Club after-school program.

Before Shirley Highway was completed (begun in 1941 and completed in 1952) memorializing Henry G. Shirley, Commissioner of Virginia Department of Highways, there was a housing development named after him. Looking down the hill from the Haley house, now Haley Park on Arlington Ridge, was the development of "Henry G. Shirley Homes", built during World War II as affordable housing.

The 1952 Sanborn Fire Insurance map shows the extensive housing development. Almost no living persons in the immediate area have any knowledge of its existence (figure 58) [61].

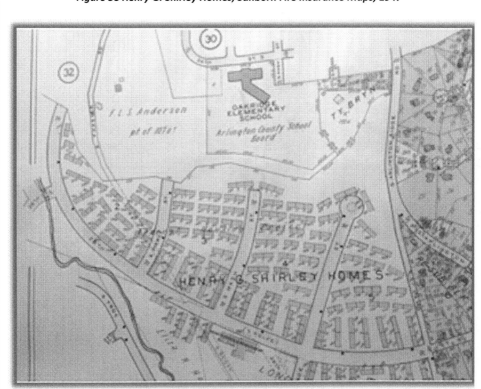

Figure 58 Henry G. Shirley Homes, Sanborn Fire Insurance Maps, 1947

Defense Homes Corporation built 26 housing projects in the United States during WWII. Five of them were dormitory or hotel projects for single persons; 21 were family dwellings, including individual homes and apartments. Of the family dwelling projects, three were in Washington, D.C. area. Three family dwelling projects were on Arlington Ridge: J.E.B. Stuart, Jubal Early, Henry G. Shirley were part of the Arlington Ridge neigborhood.

In Arlington, homes were constructed ignoring Arlington County building and zoning regulations. Residents were selected on the basis of need and segregated according to race. The Jubal Early, George Pickett, Henry G. Shirley, and J.E.B. Stuart developments were for whites. The George Washington Carver and Paul Dunbar developments were for blacks. The homes were built on concrete slabs without basements and heated by coal stoves.

In an Arlington County Library blog post[62] one former resident remembers:

> *"I know all about the Shirley homes, 1940's. This was a great place for a child to grow up, plenty of neighborhood children, more than enough to make up a ball team. Really nice people, though we were all dirt poor...never any crime there...think everyone there supported the war effort during WWII. Everybody was ordered out around 1953...later the whole place was torn down."*

In the mid-1950's the Shirley Homes development was demolished and Brandon Junior High was built in 1957 for grades 7 through 9 on the 20 acre site with the 2700 S Lang Street address.

Originally slated to be named Brandon Junior High School after the school it replaced Dolley Madison Junior High School, the name was changed in 1959 to Gunston Junior High, after Gunston Hall, the home of George Mason. The school was part of the community "lighted school program" in order to foster nighttime and weekend community use. It was determined during the 1968-1969 school year over 77,000 members of the community used the facilities (figure 59)[63].

Figure 59 Gunston Middle School Entrance

It was closed in 1978 after a major decline in enrollments and served as a South Arlington recreation center. Gunston Middle School reopened in 1994 to address overcrowding in other area schools. Funded by a year 2000 bond, it went through a major renovation project completed in 2003 making it into a two story building with a public recreation center and auditoriums.

Figure 60 Gunston Rearview and Athletic Fields

One former student remembers:

> *"I was part of the first class at Gunston when it reopened. I'm not sure what the mascot was in the past but they allowed us to vote and pick the current one. We chose the Hornets with our colors being purple and teal." And, "There were always scary stories about a guy dressed up as a clown that lurked in the woods between Oakridge and Gunston."*

Like many schools the front entrance is not what is remembered about the building. That entrance faces a hill up to Arlington Ridge. Likely only visitors enter on the "front side".

The backside of the school, with its athletic fields, tennis courts, and multiple entrances is most recognizable...and now, Charley and I don't see any "NO DOGS ALLOWED ON SCHOOL PROPERTY" signs (figure 60)[64].

Date written: 8/23/2016 revised 1/3/2020

Today Charley and I walked around Arna Valley at the south end of Army Navy Drive and South Glebe Road. Part of our walk is along Army Navy Drive, once the historic Old Georgetown Road that ran between Long Branch creek and Arlington Ridge known as: "the road from Alexandria to the ferry" (ferry at the Potomac crossing near the current Rosslyn to the mouth of Rock Creek at Georgetown). The track of the "woods path" and creek, while modified by the construction of Shirley Highway (I-395) and the Pentagon in the 1940s, are similar, though not coincident.

Today this section of road is called Army Navy Drive because it provided access to the Army Navy Country Club, founded in 1924. Arna Valley took its name from Army Navy (ARmy NAvy) Drive that, at the time the houses were built, bordered it to the west and north. The completion of Shirley Highway severed that physical connection as shown in the 1947 Sanborn Fire Insurance Map (figure 61) [65].

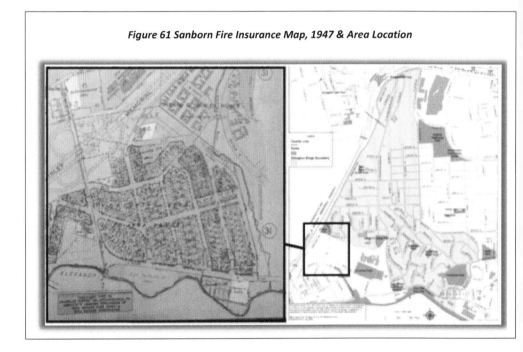

Figure 61 Sanborn Fire Insurance Map, 1947 & Area Location

The area is now a quiet, 20-acre bedroom community that is a collection of newly-constructed, multi-story townhouses, apartments and condominiums. Residents mostly commute to the Pentagon and Washington, DC jobs. Upscale now, the property has had a long and checkered history.

When we moved back to Arlington in 1990, Arna Valley was poor, but orderly. We were always surprised to see children waiting for the school bus in the morning all lined up and behaving properly. A mile away on the Ridge children were not so disciplined at the school bus stops.

The construction of the Pentagon in 1941 created a local housing demand for over 20,000 workers and their families. President Roosevelt declared that Arlington County had an acute housing shortage which would "impede war activities".

On a wooded farmland area Arna Valley became the first large-scale property in the nation constructed under the War Housing Insurance Fund and provided housing for industrial workers in 600 apartments.

Figure 62 Arna Valley Apartments

For the next 55 years the area changed little in appearance -- 66 garden-style buildings with over 600 plain brick, one-bedroom apartments divided by paved roads, lined with older-model cars. But the population morphed from the Pentagon, war-era workers to low-income, ethnic populations with a reputation for crime (figure 62) [66].

During the 1990's a bridge near Arna Valley, had the spray-painted words "La Mara Loco Intocables" -- "the crazy untouchables", a marking of a youth gang operating in Arna Valley. [67]

On the occasion of the last residents' departure, an extract from a Washington Post article based on an interview with a Mr. Hernandez, stated:

"It's a little sad," he said. "I've been here nine years, and it was home... The best thing was the low rent."[68]

Arna Valley had been an eight-block complex of inexpensive, all-brick apartments for 3,000 immigrant Hispanic families and friends who had lived there over a generation – now they would disappear.

Demolished in 2000, the apartments were replaced by The Avalon at Arlington Square condominium/apartment/stores development, The Park at Arlington Ridge apartments, Arna Valley View apartments (2001, 101 units) and Olde Forge condominiums (1984, 32 units).

The whole area is new, safe, and upscale. It is a pleasure to walk through its streets and alleys. And, there are lots of dog friends, too.

Date written: 9/6/2016 revised 1/3/2020

When I gave directions to the house that we lived in 2001-2018, I usually said, "It's the only Tudor on Nash." Because we live in a Tudor home, Charley and I decided we would try to find all the other Tudor homes in our area.

Aurora Highlands (1896 amalgamation of the original three subdivisions: Addison Heights, Aurora Hills, and Virginia Highlands) is an area that includes Arlington Ridge and much of Army-Navy Country Club. The bounds of the neighborhood are: East - S. Eads Street; North - S. 16th Street; South - S. 26th Street; and West - S. Joyce and S. Ives Streets. Historical documents state that it "...includes thirty-three Tudor Revival-style dwellings constructed between 1911 and 1940"[69]. However, a careful walk on Arlington Ridge of all streets and tally of true "Classic Tudor Revival" homes yields only 10, not 33. In fact, in the 2008 National Register of Historic Places Registration Form for the Aurora Highlands Historic District, none of the addresses, cited for Tudor Revival-style dwellings, fit the description cited in the registration.

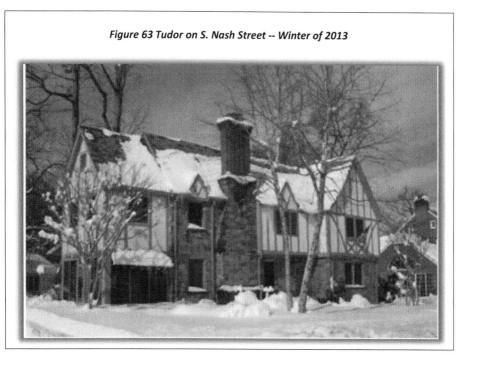

Figure 63 Tudor on S. Nash Street -- Winter of 2013

Our house was a Tudor Revival style loosely based on architectural characteristics of late Medieval English cottages and manor houses featuring Renaissance detailing. The Tudor Revival style came into prominence in the Washington metropolitan area during the late 1800's and became a widely used design during the 1920's and '30's. Tudor fell out of style during the 1940's largely due to its 'European look'. The dwellings feature large chimneys topped with decorative pots, stone or brick walls, steeply pitched parapets, steeply pitched cross-gabled roofs, elaborate facades of Gothic or Jacobean inspiration, exterior decorations such as half-timbering, skintled bricks (an irregular arrangement of bricks), and decorative stonework, and elongated windows arranged in groups with multi-pane glazing [70] (figure 63) [71].

The figure 64, below, identifies Tudor-style houses in the Arlington Ridge area.

Figure 64 Tudors of Arlington Ridge

Classic Tudor Revival				Non-Classic Tudor/Remodeled	
Address	Year Built	Address	Year Built	Address	Year Built
1404 S. 22th St	1929	2707 S. Ives St	2013	833 S. 25th St	1928
936 S. 26th St	1929	2315 S. Inge St	1937	2320 S. Ives St	1929
942 S. 26th St	1937	2707 S. Ives St	2013	2836 Ft. Scott Dr	1950
1201 S. 26th St	1937	2412 Ft. Scott Dr	1939	2511 S. Grant St	1927
1035 S. 26th St	1939	2336 S. Nash St	1935	1001 S. 26th St	1920
				2403 S. June St	1928

We originally believed the house had been built in 1938, since that was that year cited on the real estate documents when we bought the house. County records were established in 1935 so the building history before that date is not well documented.

Redoing one of the bathrooms recently we found a date of 1935 stamped on the cast iron bathtub being removed. A January 11, 1934, aerial photo shows no homes yet on what is the dirt road of what would become South Nash, originally named Forest Drive.

A 1935 map, that included the house structure (3rd house from the right on Nash Street from Woodlawn – now 23rd Road), would suggest the house was built in 1935. The detached garage didn't appear on maps until later in the 1930's (figure 65) [72].

By 1954, the Sanborn Fire Insurance maps showed jalousie additions to the house on the back and driveway sides and the addition of a garage.

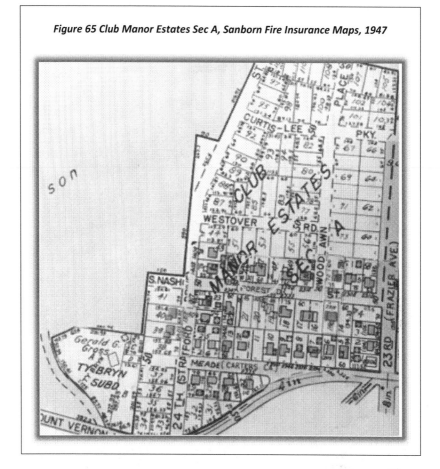

Figure 65 Club Manor Estates Sec A, Sanborn Fire Insurance Maps, 1947

Arlington County maintains a "Building Card" record for each property available at the Arlington Library Center for Local History and online (figure 66)[73].

The card for our home (Lot 47 Part 46 & 48, Section A, Club Manor Estates) catalogs the following owners:

    Maurine G. Karns 1935-1955
    Chester W. & Lorene M. Cecil 1955-1967 (Major General, USAF, retired)
    Jack S. & Bonita R. Blocker 1967-2001 (Brigadier General, USA, retired)
    Martin J. & Joyce M. Suydam 2001-2018

The card also notes a building permit 9519, dated 12/12/39: "To replace rafter, sheathing, slate cover head doors, damaged by fire."

Figure 66 Building Card for Roof Repair

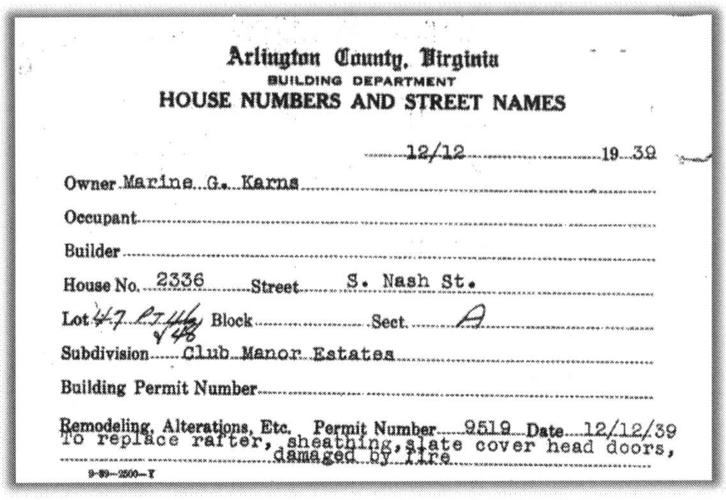

Arlington County, Virginia
BUILDING DEPARTMENT
HOUSE NUMBERS AND STREET NAMES

........12/12........ 19..39..

Owner ..Marine..G...Karns..............................

Occupant............................

Builder............................

House No. ..2336.... Street...... S. Nash St. ....

Lot 47 Pt 46 Block............ Sect....... A ....

Subdivision ....Club..Manor..Estates..............

Building Permit Number............................

Remodeling, Alterations, Etc. Permit Number ....9519.. Date...12/12/39
To replace rafter, sheathing, slate cover head doors,
...............................damaged by fire........................

9-89-2500-Y

So, what's the story of the house? What things happened in it?

All the former owners are deceased, so the "stories" may never be recorded. It is a place where they lived for 17 years and we loved it – we know that and we made changes.

We bought the house from a retired, Army Artillery general. Red is the color for artillery, so the house had lots of red – front door, front porch floor, rugs, etc. The front lawn was bordered, left and right with rose bushes (mostly red) that had been in place for nearly thirty years. Several large, old azalea bushes constituted the landscape shrubbery in the front. Many of the azaleas were salvaged, pruned and gave new life in the back yard. A large oak tree was in the driveway blocking access to the left-side garage door. The refrigerator sat in the middle of a very small kitchen (because it was too big to go against a wall). Those features were changed within the first week.

Within two years we expanded and renovated the kitchen, eliminated the back, jalousie porch, and added a breakfast room and deck. We removed the 1970's gray, veneer paneling in the basement revealing beautiful pine walls, stained mahogany. We removed the red asbestos tile floor in the basement and replaced it with a couple of thousand square feet of ceramic tile. The outside landscaping was completely changed with new, bricked areas; sodded lawn with in-ground watering system; crepe myrtle, magnolia, holly, cherry, dogwood, Japanese maple, and river birch trees; and shrubbery. We fenced in the back yard so Charley could have her own domain.

Over the next twelve years we painted and wall papered all rooms and redid all the bathrooms. We added an emergency power generator and second-floor laundry. We remodeled what was a first-floor library and added a gas fireplace. The other fireplaces were also "gasified". Its attic, with 2x10 joists and slate roof, is the "crown" to a perfect Tudor Revival house.

It has been completely modernized, but to a standard of when it was built, not "nuevo", and we loved it.

When Charley and I get back from our walks, she would always enter through the fence gate off the driveway to her backyard domain. It is her house too and she "ruled" the back yard.

Date written: 4/29/2015 revised 1/3/2020

Today is a beautiful day in February after a tough winter. We now live in Forest Hills on S. Queen Street in a townhouse about two football fields south of the location of Green Valley Manor. Charley and I walked north on Queen Street to 23rd Street (originally Fraser Street) down from the crest of Arlington Ridge.

With no leaves on the trees we could see along the center line of the road across Shirley Highway (I-395) and up into Army Navy Country Club to the small wooded knoll with the Fraser family cemetery near the golf course Blue Hole 8 (figure 67) [74]. Ignoring the intevening modern highway, hundreds of cars and trucks, and layers of fences, the view on the far side might be very similar to the view nearly 200 years ago from the original house, Green Valley Manor.

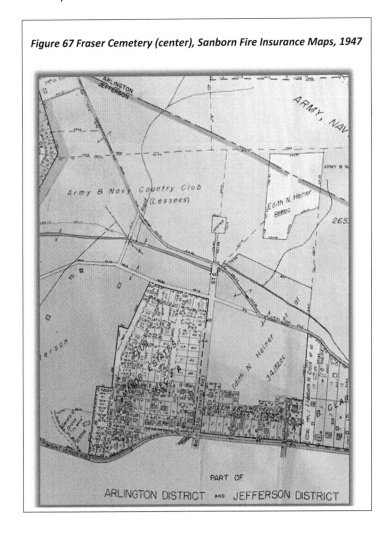

Figure 67 Fraser Cemetery (center), Sanborn Fire Insurance Maps, 1947

In the mid-1800's the Manor was a grand house with a panoramic view including the Potomac River.

Local legend has it that Green Valley Manor was named for the valley in-between a house on the facing ridge owned by James Green near the current the clubhouse at Army Navy Country Club.

Considered a mansion, the house was built by Anthony Fraser in 1821 on a 1,000 acre plantation. Even though located in Virginia, the story is that a member of the Fraser family did not believe in slavery and freed slaves providing them land and money to build their own homes. As opposed to neighbors who were imprisoned and lost most everything during the war, the Frasers faired much better.

A pencil sketch by a Union soldier, "Fort opposite Alexandria 1861", shows Fort Scott (center) and Green Valley Manor (upper left) overlooking the Four Mile Run Creek as viewed from an inlet cove (on the Potomac River (figure 68) [75].

Figure 68 Arlington Ridge, Fort Scott, & Green Valley Manor

For the Frasers of post-Civil War, Green Valley the estate was reduced to a 46-acre farm with a 2½-story "manor" residence with features, lives, and fortunes, altered dramatically by the war.

An 1865 map, noting "Fraser" and "Fort Scott", shows the approximate location (star) where the soldier-artist likely drew the picture (Potomac inlet in lower right corner of overlay). The artist must have been in a boat in the cove south of the current Reagan Airport looking northwest along the lower leg of the L-shaped high ground, now called Arlington Ridge (figure 69) [76]. The cove no longer exists having been filled in when the Corps of Engineers realigned the channels for flood protection.

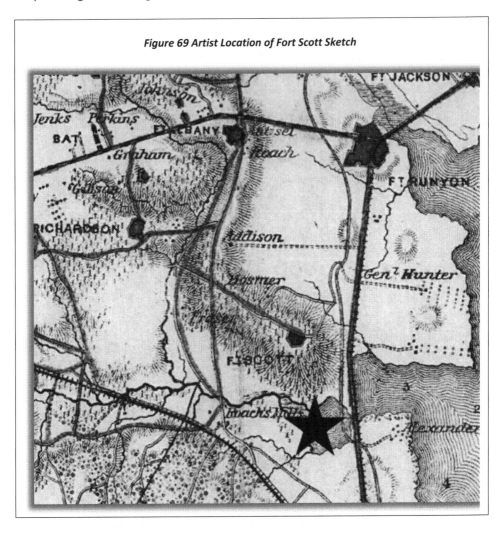

Figure 69 Artist Location of Fort Scott Sketch

It is reported that during the war Fraser's eyesight failed and being able to hear only the constant chopping of axes by Union soldiers stripping the Ridge of nearly all trees, saddened him. Today, the Ridge is wooded with grand oaks along with the "forest" of tall buildings of Crystal City. It is hard to imagine how bare it was during the Civil War.

Anthony Fraser survived the war but died in 1881 and was buried in the family cemetery. Frances Lee Sickles, the granddaughter of Fraser, inherited the property from her parents, Jackson Sickles, and Presha Antonia Fraser, and was the owner into the 20th century.

Figure 70 Green Valley Manor & Servants' House c.1915

The picture of the property (figures 70 & 71)[77], circa 1915, show two houses, an uphill view of the manor and servants' house, front view of the manor, springhouse, and barn.

Figure 71 Green Valley Manor Spring House & Barn c.1915

In a long, rambling 1915 article published in Washington Evening Star, the author, "The Rambler" describes the property at the time (extracted as figure 72).[78]

Figure 72 Green Valley Manor Description, 1915

A mile or so further down the valley, so far down that the ridge beyond Four-Mile run has changed from light, misty blue to a rich purple, you come to a place where the main road veers from the south to the southwest and a private road leads straight ahead. At this parting of the ways the Rambler pauses for a few minutes.

Down the private road can be seen through the bare branches of many oaks an old house of most substantial build and so well cared for that but for its chimneys, its dormer windows and other architectural features you might mistake it for a new house. Venerable trees grow above a well kept lawn. A neatly clipped box hedge and a lily pond at the foot of a flight of steps leading up a terrace are items in the picture. Under the trees is a rustic summer house very like that

On this estate is a spring which for a century has been inclosed by a stone springhouse. That spring has been familiar to travelers over the post road through Green valley for two centuries. George Washington, traveling over that road on horseback or in a coach, liked to stop there to drink, and there is a legend that he used to tie his horse to a persimmon tree of great age, which grows close by the spring. An interesting feature of the Green valley farm is a barn whose sides are heavy white pine planking, at least a century old and still in a well preserved condition.

is the old Fraser mansion. The Rambler spent an interesting hour there.

Anthony Fraser was the owner of this land when camps and forts covered it from 1861 to 1865. He was an old man then. He had become blind and the members of his family have told the Rambler that his greatest sorrow was to listen to the sound of hundreds of axes as Union soldiers felled the forest on his land that the fort guns might have a clear field of fire, that no cover might be afforded to the enemy and that timber might be obtained for revetments for the earthworks, for barracks for the convalescent camp close by and for many other purposes.

In that old house today lives a daughter of Anthony Fraser and his wife, who was Miss Presha Lee of Montgomery county, Md. The name of the woman is Mrs. Sickles—Mrs. J. E. Sickles, if the Rambler remembers the initials. Her daughter and her daughter's husband also live there. They are Mr. and Mrs. Herbert Carter. The house is full of old mahogany and antique rugs. Oil portraits of Frasers line the walls of one of the rooms, and a feature of the dining room is one of the white marble mantels that was taken out of the White House when changes were made in that house during the term of President Roosevelt.

In 1924 Green Valley Manor was destroyed by fire from causes that were never conclusively established. Mrs. Francis Lee Sickles[79] and her daughter, Mary Sickles, were in Paris at the time, but returned to live in the nearby servants' house. During the 1990's Joyce and I lived in a townhouse in the Forest Hills development at the location of the servants' house.

In an email exchange with Selena dePackh, the sole remaining family member with direct ancestral relationship to Green Valley Manor, she provides some insight into the state of the property after the fire:

"My mother and her mother lived in the 'servant's quarters' of Green Valley after the manor burned. My mother told a story of young vandals who came up through the golf course that she ran off with a pistol...Two eccentric women living with an elderly black butler were more or less an easy target for opportunists and bullies."

Figure 73 Army Navy Country Club and Fraser Family Cemetery

It's now four months since I started researching this story. Joyce and I played the Blue Course at Army Navy Country Club yesterday. We paused at the Fraser cemetery before teeing off on Blue Hole 8 (figure 73 star) [80] – the last physical reminder from the 1800's of the contributions of the Fraser family.

Nearly a hundred years ago the Frasers left an interesting historical legacy, however, the story of the next hundred years of Fraser family history is also interesting and remarkable, but not on Arlington Ridge.

Date written: 5/17/2015 revised 1/3/2020

A longtime resident of Arlington Ridge, Ann Donohue, remembers as a child in the 1930's how "...mean, old, Mrs. Sickles would chase them away with her shotgun and dogs". The main house of Green Valley Manor burned in 1924 while Mrs. Sickles and her daughter Mary were in England.

Francesca (Frances Lee Fraser Sickles Carter) Anderson (figure 74) [81] was living in the servants' house that remained after the main house burned. Born at Green Valley Manor, she retained her maiden name through two marriages (Anderson and Carter) although official deeds and records of Arlington would show "Frances Lee Anderson". She died in Bournemouth, Dorset, England in 1956. Her portrait is in the possession of the Arlington Historical Society. Her daughter, Mary Fraser Carter DePackh died in Pittsburgh, Pennsylvania in 1998.

An abbreviated version of the Fraser-Sickles family tree (figure 75) [82] traces the direct lineage from Anthony Fraser to the last surviving family member connected directly to the property, Selene DePackh.

Figure 74 Francis Anderson

In an exchange of emails with Selene dePackh, she revealed the following about her mother Mary and grandmother, Frances:

> *"My grandmother was institutionalized more than once as a paranoid schizophrenic, and my mother shared some of those characteristics, so a haze of questionable memories tinges my knowledge. My grandmother died at my grandfather's estate in England that she'd gotten in their divorce. She left the US to avoid another competency hearing and further loss of her independence. She died when I was a year old, and I never met her.*

Figure 75 Fraser Family Tree 1792-2020

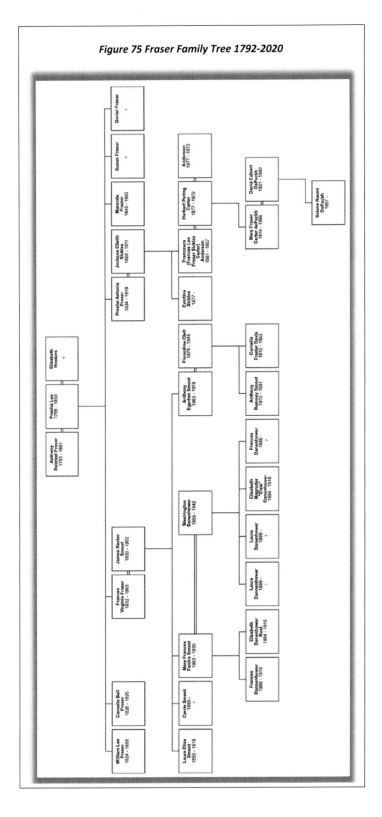

... the facts are likely to be at least as painful as they are colorful. The only direct documentation I have of my grandmother's life are some notes I found after my father's death that he took during her final US hearing, when he and my mother sought to have her declared 'non-compos mentis.' My grandmother was dependent on morphine during much of her life and was taken advantage of at many points. The family holdings were depleted to a succession of ventures, and whether or not it would have been a kindness to have taken away her liberty to preserve her assets is an open question."

After she left for England the property and its remaining buildings, under caretaker, Willie Thompson, deteriorated. Mrs. Sickles never returned. The barn burned in the 1960's along with the remaining servants' house being vandalized (figure 76) [83].

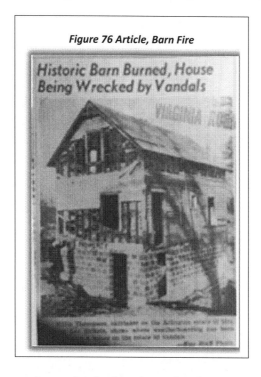

Figure 76 Article, Barn Fire

Thirty years later not much remained other than a few foundations. A neighbor, Bill White, who in the early 1960's, moved to South Pierce Street a block away from the Fraser house site, "borrowed" pachysandra that thrives today, from the Fraser house site. He remembers the site being near the intersection of the current South Queen and South Rolfe Streets.

By the 1940's the vast property that originally spanned much of today's Arlington Ridge and Army Navy Country Club had been reduced to the "Francis Lee Anderson" property shown in the map extracted from a Sanborn Fire Insurance map (figure 77) [84]. It was bounded by Army Navy Drive, South Glebe Road, Arlington Ridge Road, and the high-ground area approximately bordered by South 24th-South Pierce-South 23rd Streets. During WW II it would shrink further with Shirley and Arna Valley homes developments. The 1950's would see it shrink further with the development of Gunston Middle School campus and adjoining shopping area.

Figure 77 1935 Sanborn Fire Insurance Map of "Club Manor Estates Sec A" Overlay on Current Property Map

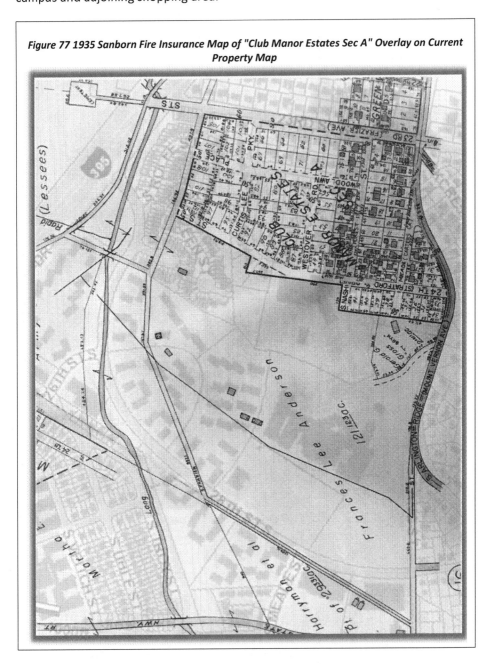

The Green Valley Manor house site remained undeveloped until the 1970's when the Forest Hills Townhouses were built on the site. As late as the 1980's it was reported that parts of the fireplace, foundation, and walls remain concealed by vegetation. If those remains did exist, then they are no longer there today. Charley and I have searched many times in vain. There are, however, remains of the barn foundations up the hill from South Queen Street (figure 78)[85] and bottom figure ("Barn" arrow identifies the location of the foundations).

Figure 78 Barn Foundation Remains and Map Location

This is sad ending for the tale of the evolution of Fraser's Green Valley. But the modern Green Valley is still beautiful and thriving. The Fraser graveyard near golf course Blue hole 8 of Army Navy Country Club still offers a picturesque view of the area of the now-gone estate.

Date written: 10/4/2016 revised 1/5/2020

Founding Familes of Arlington Ridge: Neighbors of the Frasers

When Charley and I return from walking, Joyce often asks: "Did you see any friends"?

She's referring to dog friends, but she could mean people friends, too. Surprisingly, for all the miles we walk and dogs and people we see, we might only repeat an acquaintance in 1 out of every 10 in month's time.

We often walk a circuit in the area that includes the former properties of Fraser ("Frazier"), Addison, Lacey, Graham, Gibson as shown on Civil War-era map extract (figure 79) [86]

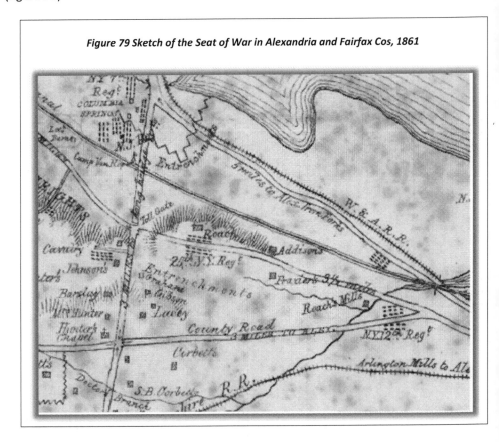

Figure 79 Sketch of the Seat of War in Alexandria and Fairfax Cos, 1861

We assume these neigbors might have been friends. However, neighbors were widely separated, Also, roads between houses were not easily traveled since they were likely either dirt (not shown on map) or crushed cinders that were dusty in summer and muddy in winter. The walking distance between Fraser and Addison homes is about a half mile, so maybe, they rarely saw one another nor had their dogs play together.

The closest Fraser neigbors were the Addisons. Since the name Addison is still in use today on the Ridge, you could expect to know more about the Addison family, but we know very little. The map shows three structures as belonging to Addison. One of those buildings was a Civil War-era white frame farm house built by Augusta Edward Addison, who owned large real estate holdings that included much of the area stretching from today's Arlington Ridge Road to the Potomac River.

In an 1917 article from a series "With The Rambler" that appeared in the Washington Evening Star newspaper, a description of The Ridge area and various neigbors is in the extract of the column as figure 80 [87].

Figure 80 "The Rambler" Article on Frasers-Addisons

of Washington. Half a mile to the south of Fort Runyon a private lane led west for three-quarters of a mile to one of the Addison homes, which stood on the east slope of the ridge south of the big brick house, still standing, of James Roach, whose important flour mills were on Four-Mile run, somewhat less than a mile west of where the railroad now crosses the run.

The name of the Addison family of that part of the environs of Washington is preserved in the name of the electric railroad station and the settlement of Addison. Half a mile south by a trifle west of the Addison place was the Fraser property, then in possession of Anthony Fraser, whose wife was Miss Desha Lee of Montgomery county, Md. The Fraser home stood, and still stands, on the west side of the ridge in that valley called Green valley, through which Long branch flows to join its waters with Four-Mile run, about a mile west of the Potomac. A quarter of a mile south of the lane which led into the Addison place was another lane leading from the Long bridge-Alexandria road into the Nellie Custis lands of Abingdon, which at the time of the outbreak of the civil war was the property of Alexander Hunter.

Addison Heights is a legally defined subdivision, named by Walter D. Addison, President of Addison Heights Realty in the late 1800's – yet, he and his Addison predecessors never appear in any 1800's census documents. Today people are still confused about community boundaries in the area (figure 81)[88].

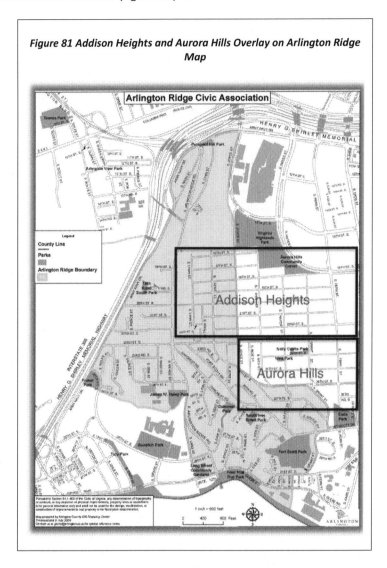

Figure 81 Addison Heights and Aurora Hills Overlay on Arlington Ridge Map

Aurora Hills was the original designation for the area now considered Aurora Highlands (figure 82)[89].

The Aurora Highlands Community Association is considered to be the eastern half of the neighborhood, while Arlington Ridge Civic Association is the western half – but there is also a popular name "Virginia Highlands" for the northwestern quadrant of the community. Regardless, Addison left an historical and mysterious imprint.

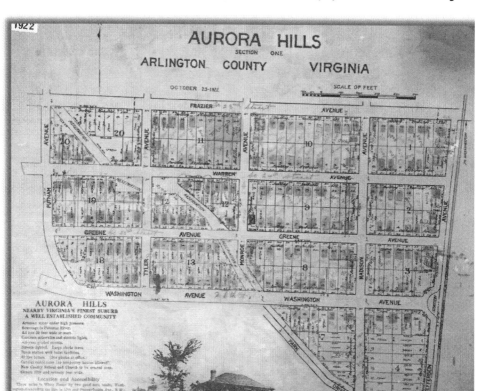

The Ridge was farm country until the 1920's. Census documents from the 1800's identify most of the the home owners as farmer or gardener, although, "Dr. A.F.A. King" was likely a physician, a distinguished title on the map. Some of the names on the map are in larger font size and often show size of property (e.g., "Ed. D. Crane, 50 a") – larger font means more acreage. While the original, early-1800's Frazier [sic] property occupied most of the area in the map extract, by 1878 much of it had been likely sold off.

Census documents offer little help for identifying these neighbors. None appear in any of the 1800's census documents. An extract of the 1860 census shows the Fraser family and identifies: Anthony, age 65, Farmer; son William, age 33, Physician; and four daughters: Cornelia, age 30; Frances, age 25; Maranda, age 21; and Antonia, age 19 (figure 83) [90].

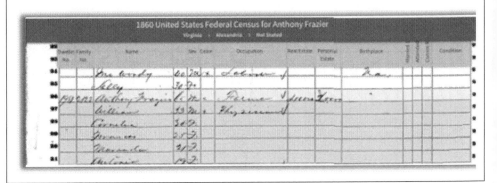

Figure 83 Extract of 1860 Census for Anthony Frazier [Fraser]

Of the 6 families mentioned earlier, only the Frasers are shown in the 1880 census, 2 years after the date of the map. So maybe neighbors didn't stay long.

Eleanor Lee Templeton's "Arlington Heritage" has the succinct citation regarding the Addisons: "On Arlington Ridge in 1900 was a subdivision called Addison Heights. The Addison house (white frame construction) appears on both 1864 and 1878 maps as on the southeast corner of what is now Ridge Road and 20th Street South was demolished in the late 1980's". [91]

Figure 84 Addison House, Sanborn Fire Insurance Maps, 1937

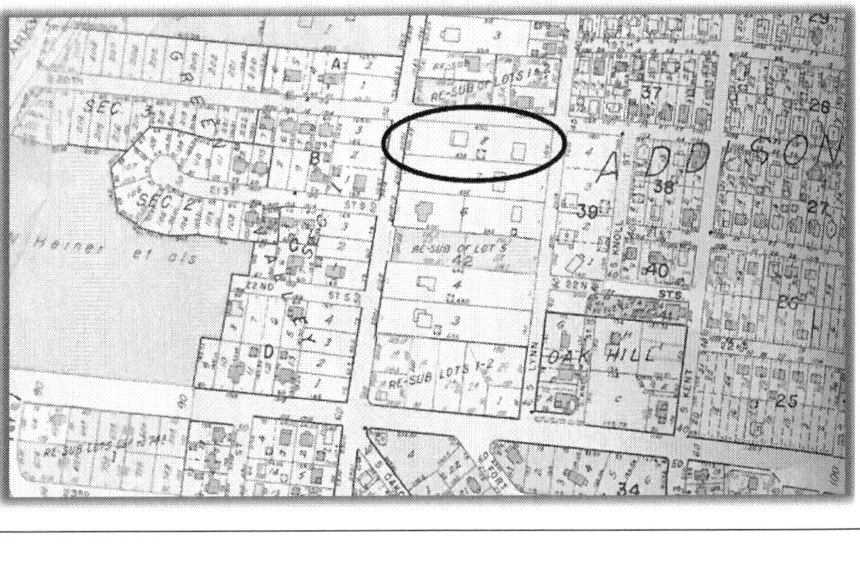

The extract from a 1937 Sanborn Fire Insurance map (figure 84) [92] identifies the house location.

The 1987 movie, No Way Out, starring Kevin Costner, opened with an helicopter view over the National Mall, the Pentagon, and Arlington Ridge Road zooming to a white frame house on the southeast corner of Arlington Ridge Road and South 20th Street, the original Addison House. A credits dispute between the then owner, Louis Pappas and the studio delayed the release of the movie. Pappas subsequently demolished the house, subdivided the lot into three parcels and built the current 3-story, brick mansion [93] (figure 85) [94].

Figure 85 Addison House, 1987 Movie, "No Way Out"

No Way Out – No more! However, Charley and I still pass by the old Addison property every day looking for neighbors and friends – people and dogs.

Date written: 10/18/2016 revised 1/4/2020

"Sunnyside Up"

The lyrics of the old Louis Armstrong song, "On the Sunny Side of the Street", "Grab your coat and get your hat -- Leave your worry on the doorstep -- Just direct your feet -- To the sunny side of the street ..."

During our early morning walks in the winter when it is cold, Charley and I would rather walk to the east toward Crystal City from Arlingtion Ridge. We like go this way because the sun warms that side of the Ridge early in the day and the other side of the Ridge is shrouded in shade and the wind seems to blow much more and much colder.

Preference to a morning sun exposure is likely why the last owners, Frank and Helen Campbell, of the Prospect Hill mansion, now a park overlooking the Pentagon, renamed the property Sunnyside.

Most of Sunnyside Farm (figure 86) [95] is today's Aurora Highlands, a residential neighborhood in Arlington, Virginia established in 1910 The area is comprised of (from north to south) the subdivisions of Virginia Highlands, Addison Heights, Aurora Hills and the Oakcrest community. During the Civil War much of this area was occuppied by Forts Albany and Scott, the beginning of the Union Army defenses of Washington known as the Arlington Line.

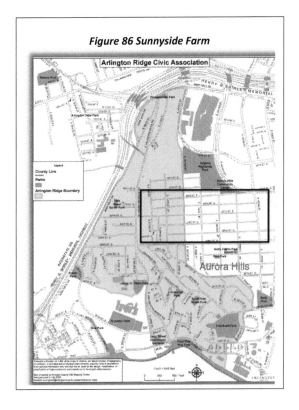

Figure 86 Sunnyside Farm

Current day Virginia Highlands and Addison Heights neighborhoods were the land of Addison Farm (or sometimes referred to as Sunnyside Farm or Sunnnydale Farm) in the 1800's.

The Aurora Highlands area was part of the Abington Plantation owned by War of 1812 General Alexander Hunter. When Hunter died in 1849, his brother Bushrod Washington Hunter was put in charge, until Bushrod's son, also named Alexander Hunter, was of age to manage the property. Starting in 1874 Hunter sold off the property in multiple parcels. Between 1876 and 1881 James Garfield, later President, was one of those who bought parcels. Frank Hume created Hume Heights in the mid-1880's, but there was little development. The area was primarily agricultural until the mid-1920's. In 1924, Frank Campbell started the Garfield Manor Corporation to develop the property formerly owned by President Garfield. Campbell subdivided the land into seven lots and recorded the plat of the subdivision under the name "Oakcrest."

Charley and I love to explore east-west-north-south streets of Addison Heights and the winding up-and-down streets and alleys and parks of Aurora Hills and Oakcrest. We even get to see some of the remaining old houses of Sunnyside.

The house at 822 South 20th Street (formerly Addison Avenue) is the only remaining structure of "Sunnyside Farm" (figure 87)[96] [97] . Constructed in 1870, the Greek Revival-style building has been altered many times, but represents the type of materials, design, workmanship of a late-1800's structure that predates the subdivision.

Figure 87 822 South 20th Street

One block east of this house is a two-story, three-bay dwelling at 721 20th Street South (formerly Addison Avenue) that was constructed in 1880 (figure 88) [98]. The building has a cross-gabled roof covered in asphalt shingles. The Italianate-style house is clad in square-butt wood shingles.

Figure 88 721 South 20th Street

In 1910 the railway stop at Addison Road (now South 20th Street) and Jefferson Street (now South Eads Street) was labeled Virginia Highlands (the collection of Arlington Ridge communities at that time). The railway ran on the towpath for the defunct Alexandria canal.

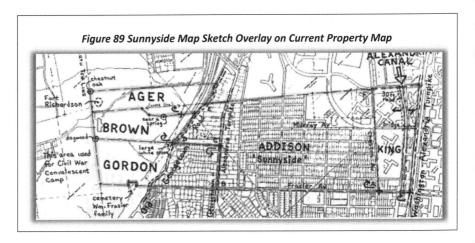

Figure 89 Sunnyside Map Sketch Overlay on Current Property Map

A property records search from the 1860 Land Book and an accompanying property map sketch (figures 89 & 90) [99] reveals details of ownership of this northeastern quadrant, 'Sunnyside', of Arlington Ridge.

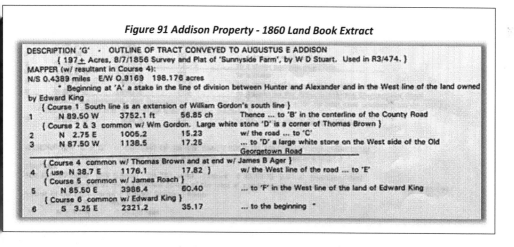

Figure 90 Sunnyside Tract - 1860 Land Book

A E Addison 197 Acres "Sunnyside" on Washington Road 4 miles NW of Cthse. Tax paid by A E Addison

Chain of Title:

Sold to Augustus E Addison by Edward B & Cordelia Powell of AlexCo and by Lawrence B Taylor and John A. Dixon of CityAlex on 8/6/1856 in R3/474 9[7]/232). Auction of 197 Acre 'Sunnyside Farm' held 4/30/1856 w/ high bid of $75/Acre or $14,775.00 total.

10 Acre portion sold to Thomas E Smithson of CityWash by Augustus E & Mary H Addison of CityBalt on 12/1/1879 in E4/130.

Last Will and Testament of Augustus E Addison of CityBalt admitted to probate there on 5/19/1881.

Devisees are widow Mary H Addison and children Walter H, Lloyd (<21), Mary and Lizzie Addison and daughter and son-in-law Sarah J and Alexander J Wedderburn.

Trustee Walter H Addison directed to sell farm in AlexCo whenever he can get $75/A.

Lis Pendens filed by Francis L Smith Attny for Samuel H Lunt against Walter D Addison Trustee to enforce a contract of sale for 187 Acre tract known as 'Sunnyside' per the cause being heard in the Circuit Court of AlexCo.

Exchange of land between Walter D Addison Trustee and the Washington Hydraulic Press Brick Co via deed dated 5/24/1895 results in net transfer of 10 Acres out of 'Sunnyside'

Sold by Walter D Addison Trustee to the Addison Heights Company, a VA corporation of a 177 Acre tract known as 'Sunnyside' on 9/14/1895 in S4/505.

Plat of a 156 Acre tract designated the 'Subdivision of Addison Heights' entered 2/15/1896 in U4/56.

Signing for the Addison Heights Company is Walter G Addison, President.

The survey description provides boundary identification with references such as: "...a large white stone on the West side of the Old Georgetown Road" (figure 91) [100].

Figure 91 Addison Property - 1860 Land Book Extract

DESCRIPTION 'G' - OUTLINE OF TRACT CONVEYED TO AUGUSTUS E ADDISON
{ 197± Acres, 8/7/1856 Survey and Plat of 'Sunnyside Farm', by W D Stuart. Used in R3/474. }
MAPPER (w/ resultant in Course 4):
N/S 0.4389 miles E/W 0.9169 198.176 acres
* Beginning at 'A' a stake in the line of division between Hunter and Alexander and in the West line of the land owned by Edward King

{ Course 1 South line is an extension of William Gordon's south line }				
1	N 89.50 W	3752.1 ft	56.85 ch	Thence ... to 'B' in the centerline of the County Road
	{ Course 2 & 3 common w/ Wm Gordon. Large white stone 'D' is a corner of Thomas Brown }			
2	N 2.75 E	1005.2	15.23	w/ the road ... to 'C'
3	N 87.50 W	1138.5	17.25	... to 'D' a large white stone on the West side of the Old Georgetown Road
	{ Course 4 common w/ Thomas Brown and at end w/ James B Ager }			
4	{ use N 38.7 E	1176.1	17.82 }	w/ the West line of the road ... to 'E'
	{ Course 5 common w/ James Roach }			
5	N 85.50 E	3986.4	60.40	... to 'F' in the West line of the land of Edward King
	{ Course 6 common w/ Edward King }			
6	S 3.25 E	2321.2	35.17	... to the beginning *

The area is bounded on the west by Georgetown-Alexandria Turnpike (now Arlington Ridge Road), on the north by a line near Clements Avenue (now South 16th Street), on the east by Cheston Avenue (now S. Fern Street), and on the south by Frazer Avenue (sometimes spelled "Frazier", now South 23rd Street),

The per acre selling price of $75 in the year 1856 would be $2,030 in 2016 – still a good deal by today's markets. However, today there are hundreds of homes that range in price from $300,000 to several millions of dollars.

It is not hard today to imagine what the area looked like up until the early 1920's – it was farm. There were a few framed houses and mostly rolling hills.

Today, Sunnyside has been developed in terms of both single-family residences and high-rise residential and commercial buildings abutting Crystal City – but still it is a nice to walk on cold winter mornings when the sun is out, so, "Grab your coat and get your hat -- Leave your worries on the doorstep -- Just direct your feet -- To the sunny side of the street -- Can't you hear a pitter-pat? And that happy tune is your step -- Life can be so sweet -- On the sunny side of the street--I used to walk in the shade -- With those blues on parade -- But I'm not afraid -- This Rover crossed over..."

Date written: 04/04/2017 revises 1/8/2020

Houses of Arlington Ridge: Disappearing Bungalows

When Charley and I walk on Arlington Ridge Road early in the morning we often meet Harry walking toward the Pentagon to the Starbacks about two miles away smoking cigarettes and wearing a very worn canvas coat and old slouch hat. Charley will see Harry at a distance and knows that Harry will always give her a treat from his coat pocket. She never gets treats during the day so this is a special meeting of very special friends.

Harry is a lifelong Arlington Ridge resident having inherited one of the two remaining bungalows on the Ridge from his parents.

The bungalow style of the United States originated in southern California and featured exposed structural features identifiable by: low-pitched front, side, cross-gable roofs, or hipped roofs with overhanging eaves and exposed rafters and decorative braces; full- or partial-width porches with full-height tapered square columns or shorter columns resting on pedestals.[101]

The two bungalows are Craftsman (Sears, Roebuck and Company of Chicago, Illinois.) homes popular in the early 1900s made available as mail-order kit-houses with complete specifications and instructions for the construction process. Sears sold 450 ready-to-assemble models that were purchased by over 70,000 American families.

Figure 92 Bungalow Locations –1934 Aerial Photograph

Both bungalows are shrouded in trees year round, but offer specular views of Washington from the backside of the house. A 1934 aerial photo of Arlington Ridge (figure 92) [102] when the road was a 2-lane divided roadway is marked with the general location of the two houses. Both were built in 1922 and have about 1800 square feet of living space. The bungalow, on the lot just south of the Hume School, appears to have been maintained well with nice landscaping (figure 93 top) [103]. Harry's, across from the intersection of Arlington Ridge Road and 19th Road, is overgrown– but it is a historical treasure that ought to be preserved (figure 93 bottom) [104].

Figure 93 1807 (top) & 1941 (bottom) S. Arlington Ridge Road

As each year passes vintage houses such as these are disappearing, making way for more expensive homes wanting to capture the ever-diminishing vistas of Arlington Ridge. We haven't seen Harry for a couple months and we miss him.

For Charley and me we like our stroll with vistas and an occassional treat, for Charley, from a nice man in an old slouch hat and worn canvas coat.

Date written: 5/3/2016 revised 1/7/2020

"Up a lazy river by the old mill run...
The lazy, lazy river in the noon day sun..."

Historically, waterways called "runs" led to the creeks and creeks entered rivers. However, Four Mile Run empties directly into the Potomac River. The whole length of the stream is named Four Mile Run and bypasses the "creek" designation by emptying directly into the Potomac River. A 2001 documentary film alleged that the name resulted from a misreading of an old map. The documentary stated that an old flour mill near the Potomac gave the stream the name of "Flour Mill Run", but the map had faded letters.

In 1624 administration of lands in the colonies was placed directly under the British crown and the governor, appointed by the crown could issue land grants.

According to the Library of Virginia:

"In 1634 the Privy Council authorized the patenting of lands under the principle of granting patents to any person who qualified as a planter. In practice, the acreage was awarded to the person who paid the transportation cost of the emigrant and not to the settler himself. This method, called the headright system, was employed as the major means of distributing virgin lands in the 17th century."[105]

The name Four Mile Run was first recorded on a land grant 1694. Grants in Colonial times were defined by reference to natural landmarks. Great Hunting Creek, south of Alexandria was such a reference point. The next sizable stream, four miles up the Potomac, hence Four Mile Run.

The documented history of the lands that include Four Mile Run begins in 1654 when the British Royal Governor Richard Bennett granted Margaret Brent, a lawyer, 700 acres including the area of Alexandria to establish a colonial-era plantation in the Chesapeake Bay area of Virginia. Originally, administration of the Virginia Colony was under the Virginia Company of London.

In 1669 Governor William Berkeley issued a 6,000-acre patent, known as the "Howson Patent", including the Brent property, to mariner Robert Howson (figure 94)[106].

Howson later sold the land to Stafford County planter John Alexander. At the time, the government required all of the large plantations to have a name, thus, the family plantation was named Caledon. After John Alexander, the father, passed away Robert Alexander inherited the upper part and his is brother, Philip Alexander, inherited the lower part of the Howson Patent tract. Several generations of Alexanders owned the tract and gradually divided it into smaller parcels. George Washington also owned a large parcel of wooded property on the southwest side of the Four Mile Run.

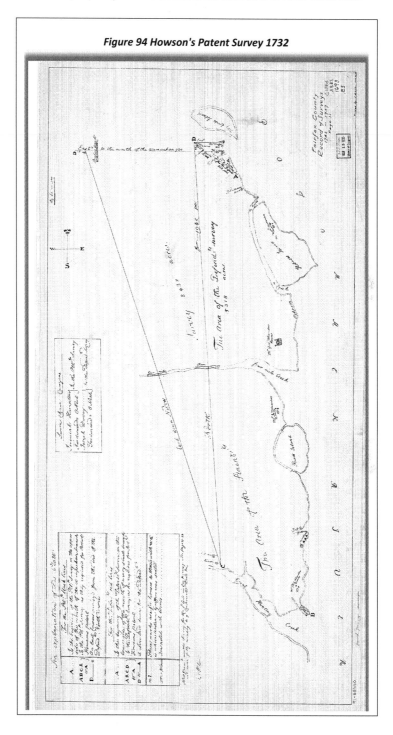

Figure 94 Howson's Patent Survey 1732

In the 1790's John Alexander's great grandsons, Edward and Ashton Alexander, held the parcel that includes Four Mile Run Park. In 1834 Anthony R. Fraser acquired their combined shares of 400 acres for his Green Valley plantation. A 1848 survey map shows the plat including roads and Long Branch stream.

Four Mile Run and its feeder, Long Branch, bound and cross, respectively, what was Green Valley, the 1,000-acre plantation and estate of Anthony R. Fraser (figure 95)[107].

The plat contains the following note: "Part of Howsin's Patent in Alexandria Co, Va called 'Green Valley' "containing, inclusive of both roads 64..2..29." Features identified are: a stream, labeled "Branch" (presumably "Long Branch"); Two roads, one road labeled "Old Road" and the other "Turnpike" (presumably what is now Army-Navy Drive and Arlington Ridge Road, respectively); a label "Scale 20 ft...Surveyed for Wm Gordon 9th Nov 1848"; and corner survey markers labeled "Post Beginning", "Stone", "2", "3", and "Small White Oak". The boundary directions and lengths are: 1) northern N88 ¾ W, 107.52 + 69.64 chains (11,692.6 feet)[108]; 2) western S9 ¼, 61.72 chains (4,073.5 feet); 3) southern S89.10, 166.20 chains (10,969.2 feet). Total area was approximately 1,000 acres.

The backside of the document is a "...Survey of Road from Tennally town Pike, through Notley Morelands a crop to & beyond Rockville & Washington Pike" -- having nothing to do with Green Valley.

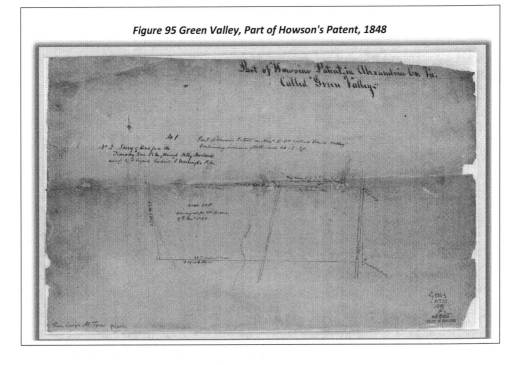

Figure 95 Green Valley, Part of Howson's Patent, 1848

During the 1700-1800's, several watermills existed in and near Four Mile Run – the only remaining foundation is Arlington Mill constructed in 1836. It was destroyed by Union troops during the Civil War and was rebuilt as Barcroft Mill in 1880. Now the foundation is part of an automobile repair shop that is located west of Four Mile Run between Columbia Pike and 10th Street South in Arlington.

One of the more beautiful and accessible portions of Four Mile Run is the Alexandria-Arlington park area near where the waterway drains into the Potomac River. This area was undeveloped through most of the 1700's to 1800's likely because it was marshy and flood prone. During the Civil War several Union Army militia units camped in the southwest portion of the park. By the late 1800's several small estates were built along what was in now Mount Vernon Avenue.

Starting in 1890, areas of the marsh began being filled for railroad, road construction and surrounding urbanization. By the late 1900's, to accommodate floodwaters, the channel was straightened, deepened, and widened. Approximately 85% of the watershed has been modified and today only 11 acres of unfilled, original tidal marsh are left.

People often believe that the waterway is 4 miles long, however, it is nearly 9-1/2 miles long. The watershed drains over 60% of Arlington County, Virginia (figure 96).

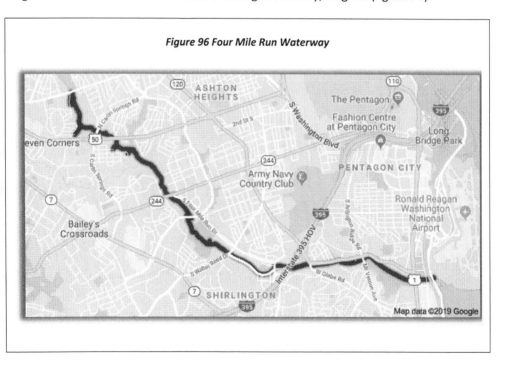

Figure 96 Four Mile Run Waterway

A September 12, 2011 Alexandria Times article[109] showed a flooded Four Mile Run Park area and reported (figure 97):

> "Serious flooding displaced residents, closed businesses and caused millions of dollars in damages with storms in 1967, Hurricane Camille in 1969 and Hurricane Agnes in 1972. Flooding linked to Hurricane Eloise in September 1975, when this photograph of Hume Springs was likely taken, caused Cora Kelly School to be shut down the rest of the year.

Figure 97 Four Mile Run Park Area Flooding Hurricane Eloise, September 1975

> To address this problem, local governments and the Army Corps of Engineers agreed to build a hardened flood control channel in the lower part of the run. The $50 million flood protection project was completed several years later and successfully prevented flooding in the adjacent communities."

The 125-year evolution from farm and swamp to urban park of the park is portrayed in figure 98[110]. Today's park area is outlined in red and transposed on each map or aerial photo – the majority of change happened since 2000.

Figure 98 Four Mile Run Park - 100 Years of Change

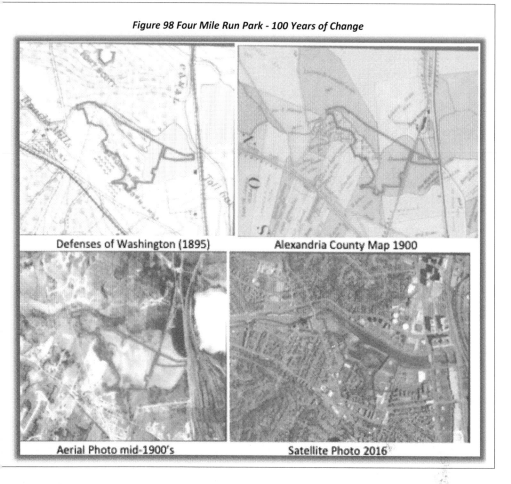

Defenses of Washington (1895) Alexandria County Map 1900

Aerial Photo mid-1900's Satellite Photo 2016

Today's Four Mile Run Park is 48-acres and is the largest suburban park in the DC area. The park includes a freshwater tidal estuary and marsh. The Hume Springs and Sunnyside tributaries cross the south side of the park to enter Four Mile Run (figure 98). It is a multi-use park area with bike-walking trails, baseball field, playground, and wildlife sanctuary.

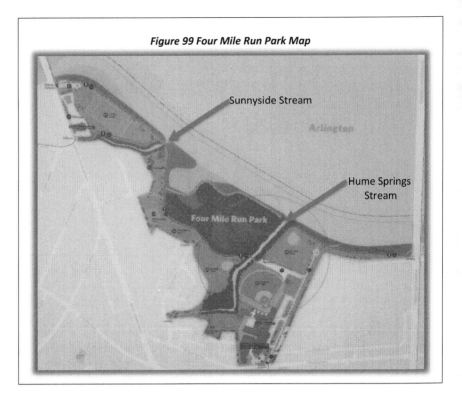

Figure 99 Four Mile Run Park Map

Four Mile Run is the Green Valley of Arlington and Alexandria.

> *"Up a lazy river by the old mill run...*
> *The lazy, lazy river in the noon day sun..."*

Date written: 12/10/19 revised 1/5/2020

Green Valley: Antebellum

Charley and I walked along Four Mile Run today. It is a hot summer day and the tall trees along stream offered shade. For the many times I have walked near Four Mile Run I had always assumed the name was derived from its length. River lengths change since the channels naturally change over the years. But rivers and streams also are changed through the work of man, as in the case of Four Mile Run, the Corps of Engineers aligned and protected the stream following Hurricane Agnes in 1972.

In antebellum Arlington (1860), the tracks of the predecessor of the Washington and Old Dominion Railroad were laid along the stream's length in Arlington.

Green Valley was created by Four Mile Run and its feeder streams: Lubber Run, Long Branch (upper), Doctors Run, Lucky Run, and Long Branch (lower). Four Mile Run is the low part of Fraser's Green Valley and exits into the tidal Four Mile Creek and then the Potomac River (figure 100)[111].

There are several theories on the name origin, from a misreading of a faded map identifying "Flour Mill Run", to it being four miles upriver from Hunting Creek in Alexandria on the Potomac. Regardless, stream length had nothing to do with its name.

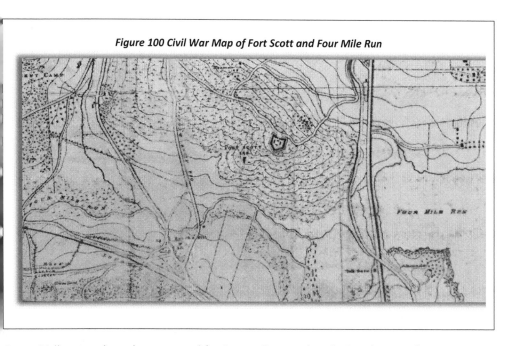

Figure 100 Civil War Map of Fort Scott and Four Mile Run

Green Valley may have been named for James Green who, during the 1700's, is recorded as living near what became the site of today's Army Navy Club clubhouse.

On the other hand, it was likely that it was simply a beautiful green valley and not named, borrowing the name from other plantations in England.

At the time Washington City was established in the late 1700's, the portion of land ceded from Virginia was Alexandria County. The Town of Alexandria was the seat of local government and commercial center. Nan and Ross Netherton in their 1987 book, "Arlington County in Virginia: A Pictorial History" wrote:

> 'The Arlington area, known as "the country part of the county," continued to have an agricultural character with a few relatively large plantations – such as Abington, Arlington, and Green Valley – the rest consisting of small landholdings worked by yeoman farmers and tenants...continued to be the grain-grower and green-grocer for Alexandria and, later, the city of Washington. The products of its farms included corn, wheat and rye, some livestock, dairy products and market garden crops. Cordwood and timber boards and barrels came from the forested hills.'

William Fraser Sr.[112] in 1758, and William Fraser Jr., in 1804, leased land in Green Valley from Walter Stoddard Alexander.

His son Anthony Fraser (1793-1881), made the transition from lessor to owner acquiring approximately 1,000 acres including parts of Four Mile Run and Long Branch Creek. He built Green Valley Manor in an oak forest in 1821 on the rising hillside, Arlington Ridge, east of the creek.

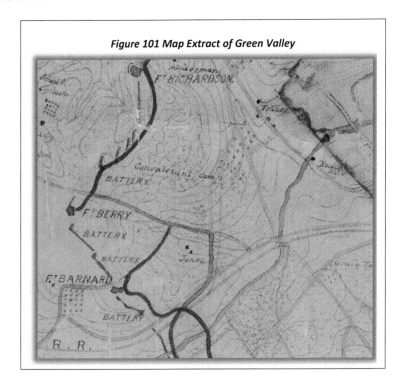

Figure 101 Map Extract of Green Valley

Figure 101[113] portrays the Green Valley area at the beginning of the Civil War.

The area shown in the map extract is about 75% of Fraser's property in Green Valley. While labeled "Convalescent Camp", it had not been constructed at the time the map was made. The following homeowners are identified: Beidermann (east of Fort Richardson), Fraser (lower right, east of "Convalescent Camp"), and Addison (upper, right border). The regular pattern trees are orchards; Other trees likely to be oaks, all which were cut down during the war for fortifications, fields of fire, and firewood; And, tufts symbols, grassland and pasture.

The catalog of data from successive census is useful in documenting not only the changes in how census was reported, but how the Fraser family and name spelling changed over time. A couple of these records are repeated from earlier stories, but are presented here to demonstrate change.

The first US Census, 1790, listed William Fraser household with 3 white souls, 1 dwelling and 3 outbuildings[114].

The 1840 census added significant detail over prior census and reported the following for Anthony Frazer [sic] (figures 102 & 103)[115]:

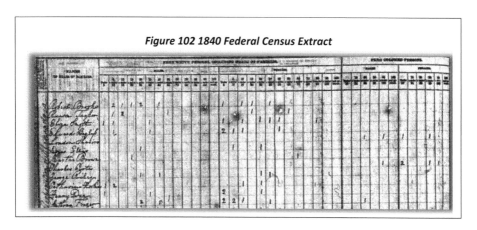

Figure 102 1840 Federal Census Extract

Figure 103 1890 Federal Census Extract Detail

Free White Persons - Males – 20-29:2; 40-49:1
Free White Persons - Females - Under 5:2; 5-9: 2; 10-14:1; 30-39:1
Free Colored Persons - Males – 24-35: 1
Slaves - Males – 55 99: 1 Slaves – Females – 10-23:1
Persons Employed in Agriculture: 4

The 1860 Census reports Frazier [sic] as a farmer, living at building number 1981, Jefferson District, Alexandria County, Virginia. His property and possessions were worth $40,000 and $20,000, respectively, about $1.2 million and $0.6 million today – assuming inflation only, but the real worth of Green Valley is many times that. In the same census, the "Lee, RE" property was worth $60,000 (figure 104)[116].

Figure 104 1860 Virginia Census Extract

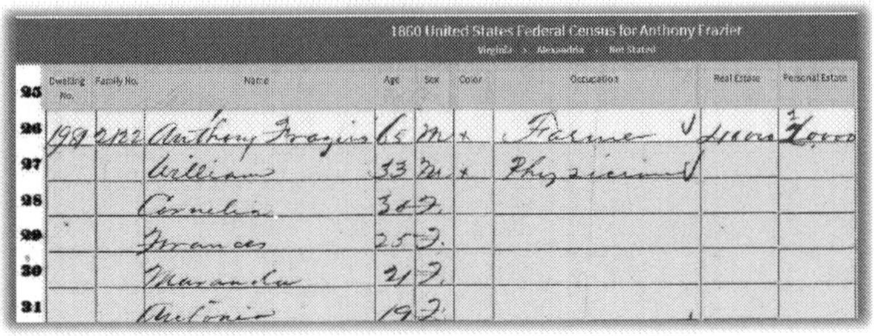

By 1880, the census reported only five people living at the residence (figure 105)[117].

Figure 105 1880 Virginia Census Extract

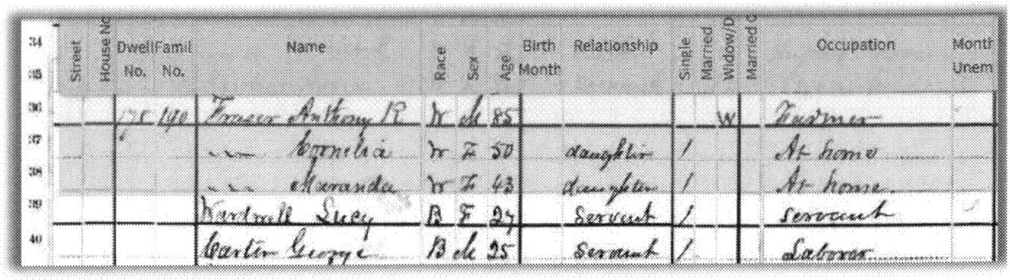

With the onset of the Civil War, Antebellum Green Valley, would lose much of its "green" -- the hills were stripped of trees. It became a site of a large convalescent center treating war wounded.

Today the area has returned to be a vulnerable green valley existing in an encroaching urban sprawl.

Charley and I enjoy the shade in the trees along Four Mile Run and we now have a better perspective about the area we love to walk. I can't wait for tomorrow when Charley causes me to think deeply about some other bit of history on our walk.

Date written: 8/6/2018 revised 1/6/2020

I'm not much of a golfer, but I do live close to Army Navy Country Club in Arlington, Virginia and I am a member. The club course and clubhouse of today are located on property that once belonged to Anthony Fraser. At the outset of the Civil War Union forces occupied the Fraser plantation establishing Fort Richardson on the high point of the Ridge.

The view from Fraser's house was of his plantation, Green Valley, including a view of what would be his family graveyard at the end of Fraser Avenue, now South 23rd Street and the Convalescent Camp (figure 106)[118].

Figure 106 Convalescent Camp (viewed along East and West Avenues)

Author Benjamin Cooling commenting on the New Convalescent Camp noted:

> *"The second Camp Convalescent was located south of Fort Richardson in the valley. The camp replaced the infamous "Camp Misery" which was located on the slopes of Shuters Hill northeast of Fort Ellsworth near Alexandria. The camp was moved to this site and constructed in 1862."* [119]

A detail map of the camp identifies hospitals and wards, barracks, officers' quarters, and administrative buildings; parole and distributing camps; and streets, trails, and railroad siding. Fort Richardson is not shown but would be above the rectangular barracks and quarters area (figure 107) [120].

Figure 107 Extract of Map of New Convalescent Camp

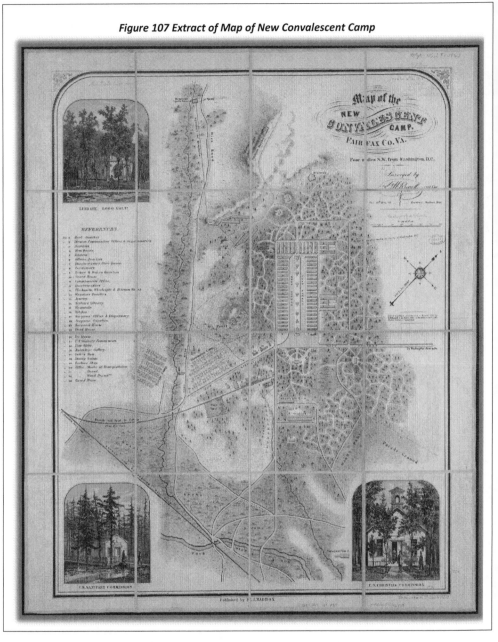

The author of the history of the Eleventh Regiment, Rhode Island Volunteers, described the second camp:

> "The present camp is in a filthy condition, and a shame to those who have charge of it. The camp was originally located about two miles nearer Alexandria, in the region

of what was called the Distributing Camp. When we took possession of Camp Metcalf they were located in the Green Valley. What was filthy before we went there, by the middle of February had become clean, and a very different affair from what it was when the government established it. It was under entirely different regulation. It grew rapidly from a small number to a moderate sized army, and what had been confusion soon became order and system." [121]

The camp was established as a hospital and recovery area for wounded convalescents returning to their commands. In January of 1864, the camp was reorganized under the name "Rendezvous of Distribution Camp" adding a stragglers' camp, a camp for drafted men and recruits, and a paroled prisoners camp. In addition to providing manpower serving the various Union Army units stationed in the defenses of Washington, the Army Engineers used the men in the construction of the fortifications in the defenses of Washington.

The Convalescent Camp occupied most of the Army Navy Country Club golf course area as shown in the "Barnard View" map[122] (Figure 108). Green polygons represent location and size of Fort Richardson, top-left, and Fort Albany, lower right, respectively (note: Shirley Highway, I-395, black line added for modern-day reference). The map extract is centered on Fraser's Green Valley Manor. The location of the picture taken identifying the US Sanitary Commission (Figure 109) [123] is near the road leading up to Fort Richardson, top center of Barnard map. [124]

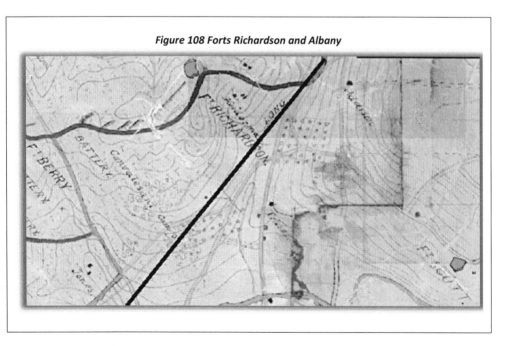

Figure 108 Forts Richardson and Albany

The camp was organized into three divisions (Division 1 - Convalescents; Division 2 - Distribution; Division 3 – Paroled) each division had four sections (Section 1 - New England, Section 2 -New York, Section 3 - Pennsylvania and "Southern", Section 4 - Western troops).[125]

An article in The Soldiers' Journal, a newspaper published at the camp, stated:

"The government sent to this camp all stragglers, all detailed privates, all the men fit for duty at Camp Convalescent, and thence they were sent in large squads to their respective regiments. There were from five to eight thousand men then in the camp. The post was under the command of Capt. Upham. Contiguous to this camp was a camp of recruits, also under the commandant of that post. Still nearer Alexandria, and distinct from the Distribution Camp, was the camp of paroled 'prisoners, containing not more than five or six hundred men; and we learned that somewhere between Camp Metcalf and Fairfax Seminary, was a convalescent horse camp, where horses that had been under medical treatment and were on the road to sound health, were treated to further rest and a fat pasture."

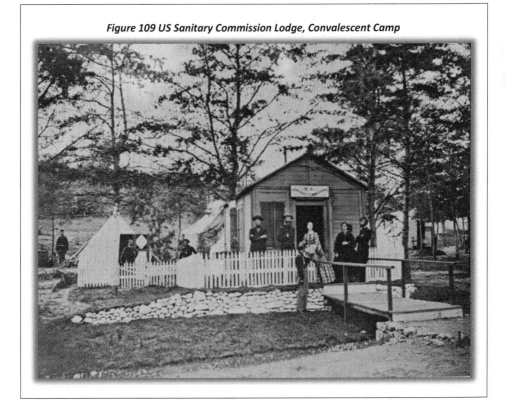
Figure 109 US Sanitary Commission Lodge, Convalescent Camp

The 50 hospital wards were nothing like modern military wards. Usually there would be two rows of beds with a wide aisle. Following battles with large numbers of wounded, beds would be added allowing only limited aisle movement (figure 110) [126].

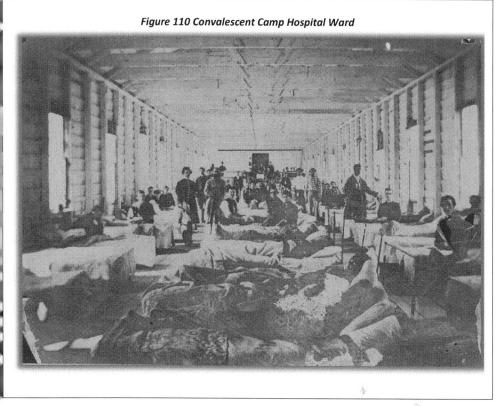

Figure 110 Convalescent Camp Hospital Ward

One of the early The Soldiers' Journal newspapers, published at the camp, catalogued the impressive production activity of the Convalescent Camp. Of 117,400 convalescents, 84% were returned to units.

A report included in the Journal for the period September 1862-December 1863 is shown in Figure 111[127], next page.

Figure 111 The Soldiers' Journal Extract

kitchens and dining rooms has a force of over forty feet, and can supply forty thousand gallons of water per day. It also supplies the barracks with water in case of fire or accident in camp.

CAMP OF DISTRIBUTION.

Camp of Distribution (a section of Convalescent Camp,) is situated a short distance from Convalescent Barracks, and inside the lines of the command. The camp is composed of Sibley tents—each tent having a Sibley stove. The camp is for the reception of men found fit for duty in Convalescent Camp, duty men arriving from Washington depots, Provost Marshals, deserters arrested by Provost Marshals, &c. The arrangements of camp are as follows: The streets or divisions of camp are divided off into Army Corps, viz: "The regiments that are serving in the various corps of the army." Each corps street is under charge of a non-commissioned officer. As fast as men arrive in camp and their names recorded by the Sergeant Major they are distributed to the corps in which their regiments are serving. The deserters are in a separate camp from the duty men, under charge a commissioned officer.

Major W. H. Wood, 17th U. S. Inf., Assistant Provost Marshal General, Army of the Potomac, sends to camp almost daily for the men of the various corps—who has the forwarding of said men to the Provost Marshal General, Army of the Potomac, for distribution to their respective regiments, and to army corps in said army. A roll accompanies the men, stating the name, company and regiment of each man, made out separately by brigades. By this means the Provost Marshal General has little or no trouble, after receiving said men, in their distribution to brigades of the army.

I think over ten thousand deserters were received at this camp and forwarded to regimental commanders for disposition. The machinery of this camp is in such working order that if called upon, from two to four thousand men can be forwarded to their regiments in one day, with the proper rolls.

Lieut. F. T. Stewart, 28th Ohio Vols., the commandant of the camp, has displayed the qualifications of an officer fully competent to meet the demands of the service, always vigilant and active in the discharge of his many duties. He is eminently entitled to the consideration of the government for promotion.

Annexed will be found a report of this camp.

In conclusion, Colonel, I would state from experience, having had the honor of being associated with Capt. R. P. Crawford, your Assistant Adjutant General, with his natural business qualifications, and his executive military talent, he has aided and assisted you greatly in the formation and organization of Convalescent Camp. He has many warm and steadfast friends.

To you, Colonel, the service owes the formation of one of the best disciplined and organized corps in the country. As the Department is fully aware of your services as an officer, I trust a speedy promotion may follow.

As over the major portion of this history is taken from memory, it is with pleasure I offer it to you, as the doings of a boy.

With high regards, &c., I am, sir,
Your most obedient servant,
H. J. WINTERS,
Chief Clerk, Commissary Dep't.

CONSOLIDATED REPORT OF CONVALESCENT CAMP, From September, 1862, to December 31, 1863. Number of convalescents admitted, - 117,405

Number of convalescents sent to join their regiments, - - - 96,293
Number of convalescents transferred to general hospitals, - - - 5,565
Number of convalescents discharged the service on Surgeon's certificate of disability, - - - 2,781
Number of convalescents furloughed, - 1,993
Number of convalescents died, - - 208
Rejected conscripts and substitutes received in this camp, having been pronounced unfit for active service, about - - - 600
Number of men assigned to the Invalid Corps at this camp, from August 1, 1863, to November 30, 1863, - 4,027
Number of paroled prisoners in camp from May, 1863, to August, 1863, - 3,084
Number of officers ordered to report to Convalescent Camp by the Military Governors of Washington and Alexandria, who were forwarded to their regiments, August 23, '62, to September 30, '63, - 342

CONSOLIDATED REPORT OF CAMP OF DISTRIBUTION From May, 1863, to December 23, 1863.
Number of men received, - - - 33,458
Number of men sent to join their regiments, - - - - 31,071
The balance are awaiting transportation to their regiments.

Amount of savings in rations to the Government, in Convalescent Camp (alone,) from June to December 1, '63 - - - $25,604 29
The above amount was not drawn in money, but is due this camp.

BATTLE OF GETTYSBURG.—This battle of three days will compare in magnitude and far-reaching consequences, with any of the great battles of modern times. In the battle of Waterloo, the Allies had 72,000, the French 80,000 men; in this the rebels had 90,000 the Federals about 60,000 men. The British had 186 cannon, the French 252; the rebels had upwards of 200, and we an equal number. The Allies lost 22,000 in killed and wounded; the French 40,000 in killed, and wounded, prisoners, and deserted; the Federals lost about 4,000 killed, 12,000 wounded and 4,000 prisoners or in all about 20,000; whilst the rebels lost 5,500 killed, 23,000 wounded and 9,000 prisoners and 4,000 stragglers and deserters, or a total of about 40,000. The proportion of men and of losses in both battles is nearly the same. In this battle 28,000 muskets were taken. Of these 24,000 were found to be loaded, 12,000 containing two loads, and 6,000 from three to ten loads each. In many instances half a dozen balls were driven in on a single charge of powder. In some cases the former possessor had reversed the usual order, placing the ball at the bottom of the barrel and the powder on top.

Gov. BROWN, of Ohio, recently observed a young officer in the streets of Columbus grossly intoxicated. He telegraphed to the Secretary of War for his removal, and by the time the young man recovered his sobriety he found his commission vacated; nor could the possessions of influential friends change the determination of the Governor, who declared that, as President of a railroad company, he had made it a rule to dismiss any employee subject to intoxication, and he could not deviate from that rule in a case where the offender was intrusted with the care of men.

[From the
A Visit to
United S

Anecdotes from reports and letters offer an insight into camp life, as follows:

"Unfortunately, when the men from the Convalescent Camp worked on the fortifications, they rarely did good work. Superintendent Clark reported on October 19, 1863, that "Mr. Hawkins reports that details of 212 men from the Convalescent Camp done the work of about 20 laborers. The officers informed him that their instructions were to bring the men out, not to make them work." Clark reported, on October 20, 1863, that the detail of 225 men from the Convalescent Camp wouldn't work and that the officers could not compel them to do so. On October 22, 1863, Alexander informed the Chief of Staff of the Department "You will perceive that Mr. Clark still says that the men from the Convalescent camp do not work properly." [128]

Actually, the convalescents' work improved considerably if a sufficient and competent guard, with good officers, accompanied them. Clark reported on November 6, 1863 that a small detail from the Convalescent Camp reported for work that day because the guard left about 3 a.m. "when there was a general stampede out of Camp." Alexander felt that "a competent officer should be placed in command with a guard strong enough to enforce his orders, and that he is instructed that it is his special duty to see that the men are kept at work." One soldier reminisced: "Guard duty at Convalescent Camp began at once on Thursday, the 15th, and the men were on duty every other day, either at that camp, the new barracks, not then finished, or our own camp. The service was a heavy one, and the men began to see that there was work to be done more wearing than going to the front." [129]

Date written: 7/23/2018 revised 1/8/2020

In June of 2018 Joyce, Charley and I moved back to the Forest Hills townhouses. Now, when Charley and I take our daily walks, we pass directly over the land that was the site of Green Valley Manor. Except for the very busy Shirley Highway corridor that runs up the valley toward the Pentagon, the area is beautiful with treed and grassed hillsides – it is a Green Valley.

In the early 1800's father and son James and Anthony Fraser acquired many parcels that became the 1,000-acre Green Valley estate. Figure 112[130] documents a chain of title for a few (of the many) 40+ acre parcels transferring ownership from the early settler/owners, Alexanders, to Frasers.

Figure 112 Chain of Title, Fraser Property

Chain of Title:
- 40 A sold to James Frazier of AlexCo by Austin & Eleanor Alexander on 8/2/1826 in P2/418 {[3]/139}.
- 46+ A sold to James Frazier by George D Alexander on 2/2/1828 in Q2/481 {[3]/227}.
- 48+ and 40 A tracts both sold to Anthony R Fraser of AlexCo by James & Mary Ann Fraser of AlexCo on 2/23/1833 in U2/426 {[3]/501}.

After the Civil War Green Valley returned to life as a quiet farm. The hillsides had been stripped of trees, and buildings, hospitals, convalescent camp and forts were demolished, and Long Branch ran clear water. The Fraser family resumed their farm life and Green Valley became secluded and forested. While the Frasers had been major landholders in Alexandria County, over time, the property maps show a patchwork of many owners.

After the Civil War, Green Valley property was gradually subdivided many times. Figure 112[131] documents a few multiple transfers of property up through the early 1920's. By then the various tracts morphed from separate farms to a large golf course and other residential and commercial developments.

By 1900 the estate had been subdivided and was now reduced to 150 acres with some parcels held by family members such as daughter, Antonia F. Sickles.

Eleanor Lee Templeton in her book "Arlington Heritage", stated, "At the mansion's site I found traces of the terraced woodland garden where daffodils still bloom, and the masonry steps leading down to the cup of a fish pond or fountain."[132] Another Arlington historian, C (Cornelia).B. Rose Jr., wrote in a newspaper column, "Between the end of the War Between the States, and twentieth century progress, Green Valley enjoyed about a half century of rural peace, and was described in 1887 as "secluded" and "not without picturesque pastoral beauty." Green Valley was again a farm or plantation, no longer a busy hospital and convalescent center.

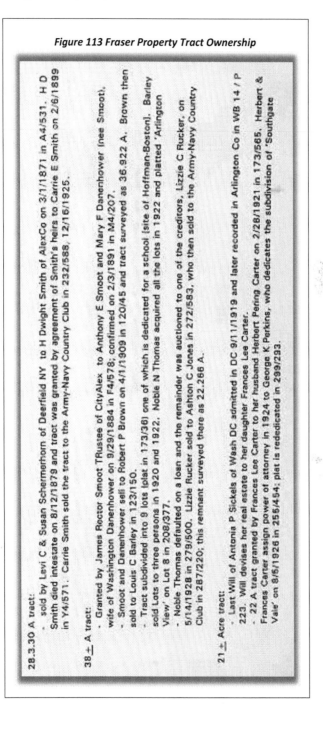

Figure 113 Fraser Property Tract Ownership

28.3.30 A tract:
- sold by Levi C & Susan Schermerhorn of Deerfield NY to H Dwight Smith of AlexCo on 3/1/1871 in A4/531. H D Smith died intestate on 8/12/1879 and tract was granted by agreement of Smith's heirs to Carrie E Smith on 2/6/1899 in Y4/571. Carrie Smith sold the tract to the Army-Navy Country Club in 232/588, 12/16/1925.

38 ± A tract:
- Granted by James Rector Smoot TRustee of CityAlex to Anthony E Smoot and Mary F Danenhower (nee Smoot), wife of Washington Danenhower on 9/29/1884 in F4/578; confirmed on 2/3/1891 in M4/207.
- Smoot and Danenhower sell to Robert P Brown on 4/1/1909 in 120/45 and tract surveyed as 36.922 A. Brown then sold to Louis C Barley in 123/150.
- Tract subdivided into 9 lots (lost in 173/36) one of which is dedicated for a school (site of Hoffman-Boston). Barley sold Lots to three persons in 1920 and 1922. Noble N Thomas acquired all the lots in 1922 and platted 'Arlington View' on Lot 8 in 208/377.
- Noble Thomas defaulted on a loan and the remainder was auctioned to one of the creditors, Lizzie C Rucker, on 5/14/1928 in 279/500. Lizzie Rucker sold to Ashton C Jones in 272/583, who then sold to the Army-Navy Country Club in 287/220; this remnant surveyed there as 22.266 A.

21 ± Acre tract:
- Last Will of Antonia P Sickels of Wash DC admitted in DC 9/11/1919 and later recorded in Arlington Co in WB 14 / P 223. Will devises her real estate to her daughter Frances Lee Carter.
- 22 A tract granted by Frances Lee Carter to her husband Herbert Pering Carter on 2/28/1921 in 173/565. Herbert & Frances Carter assign power of attorney in 1924 to George K Perkins, who dedicates the subdivision of 'Southgate Vale' on 8/5/1926 in 255/454; plat is rededicated in 299/293.

Arlington Land Ownership in 1900 is catalogued in an ownership map used by Arlington County to portray modern streets and facilities (figure 114).[133]

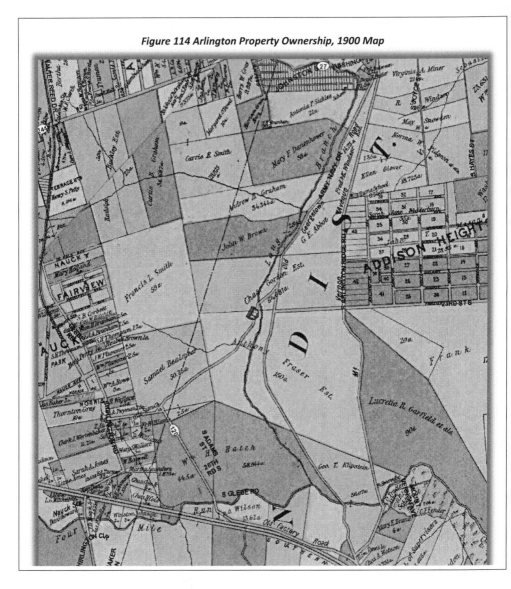

Figure 114 Arlington Property Ownership, 1900 Map

Today, Green Valley is dominated by the Army Navy Country Club, Forest Hills Townhouses, and most of the communities that comprise Arlington Ridge.

Green Valley Manor was destroyed by fire in 1924. In that year Army Navy Country Club was founded on the property west of Army Navy Drive (that traces the approximate route of the Old Georgetown Road). The groundbreaking for the clubhouse, by the Army Chief of Staff and Marine Corps Commandant was in 1927 as feature in a Washington Post article Figure 115[134].

Figure 115 Army Navy Marine Corps Clubhouse Ground Breaking

Most traces of the Green Valley mansion property, its manor, servants' house, outbuildings, foundations, springhouse, smokehouse, were obliterated when the Forest Hills Townhouses were built in the 1970's and the hillside was stripped of trees (figure 116)[135].

Figure 116 Forest Hills Townhouses Under Construction -- early 1970's (north-looking view)

In 2020, we can view Green Valley from space using Google Earth. Trees and beautiful landscaping present a view worth preserving -- a beautiful green valley that Anthony Fraser left as a legacy, and a family gravesite allows a grand view (figure 117)[136].

Figure 117 "Green Valley 2020"

Date written: 8/20/2018 Revised 1/8/2020

From Trolley Park to Sewage Treatment: Luna Park

Sometimes Charley and I take a long walk around the perimeter of Arlington Ridge. We walk south to the trail alongside Four-Mile Run, then east to South Eads Street, then north on Eads. That last corner is now is part of the Arlington County sewage treatment facility, a very large, modern, waste processing operation that also includes drop-off locations for hazardous waste (figure 118) [137].

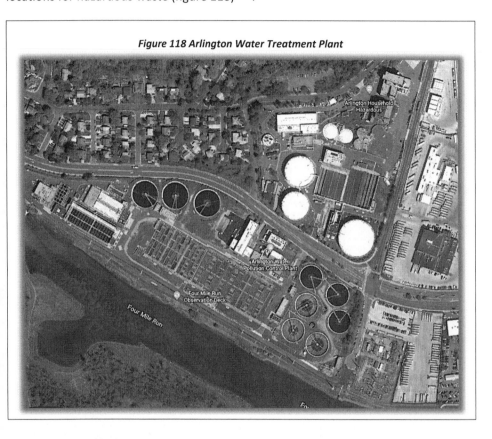

Figure 118 Arlington Water Treatment Plant

In the early 1900's there was a 34-acre "trolley park", Luna Park, on that property (figure 119) [138]. The trolley park got its name from the fact that it was located along an electric-powered inter-urban trolley line that provided easy, affordable transportation for Washington and Alexandria along the route of the old Georgetown-Alexandria canal. The original canal structures are gone, but the Washington Metrorail system now follows the canal's route. The location where the canal crossed over Four Mile run was the site of an explosive train wreck that occurred in 1885 where the canal, train tracks and wagon road (now US 1) intersected at the Four Mile run crossing.

Figure 119 Washington Luna Park, Arlington, Virginia

Trolley parks were the precursor to amusement parks and were fostered by the streetcar companies to make use of the transportation on weekends. The Washington Times of recorded[139].

> "The normal fee for the round trip on the line was twenty-five cents but the railway offered a special rate of fifteen cents to entice park patrons from both the Washington and Alexandria terminals."

Luna Park had a figure-eight roller coaster, circus arena, ballroom, chute-the-shoots slide, restaurants and picnic facilities for 3,000 people as noted in an original map sketch of the park (figure 120)[140]. There were other short-lived parks named Luna Park in North America (Pittsburgh, Cleveland, Scranton, and Mexico City), all developed by Frederick Ingersoll, mostly with shaky finances.

Figure 120 Luna Park Facility Layout

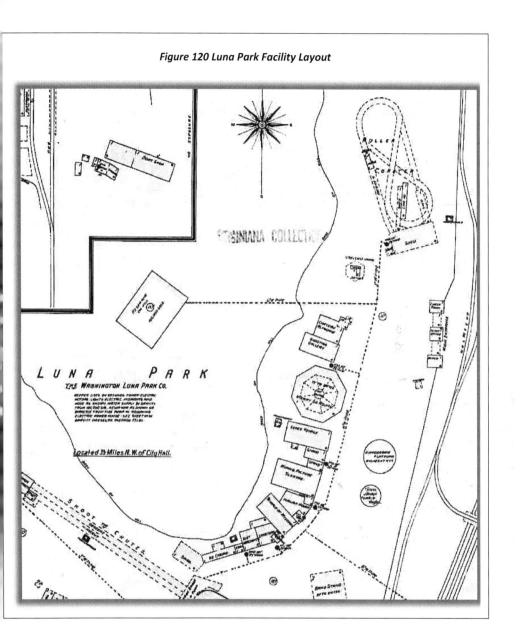

The Alexandria Gazette of August 16, 1906 carried the following article:

"Several elephants which are to be exhibited at Luna Park next week are expected to arrive via the Baltimore & Ohio Railroad. They will be led through the city on their way to the resort. Luna Park, which has been a decided success from the day it opened, grows in popularity and continues to be visited by thousands."

Later the Alexandria Gazette reported that:

"On the morning of August 21st, the four elephants, a male whose name was Tommy and three females, Queenie, Annie, and Jennie, escaped. Annie was quickly caught. The others headed toward Alexandria where they smashed a barn, decimated a cornfield, and trampled a graveyard. By nightfall, Tommie had been caught and owner P.W. Barlow was offering a $500 reward for the capture of Queenie and Jennie. He persuaded Maj. Gordon W. Lillie to dispatch some of his men after the pair. Lillie was in town with "Pawnee Bill's Wild West and Great Far East Exhibition." When he put on his red cowboy shirt, he became Pawnee Bill.

Still later the Alexandria Gazette reported that:

"On Sunday, August 26th, a horse-mounted procession set off from Alexandria toward Baileys Crossroads, where there had been an elephant sighting. They found Jennie in a thicket and a "Wild West" performer named "Mexican Joe" lassoed her. Queenie remained the last holdout at large... She was captured the next night by Barlow and his men in a pine grove 20 miles south of Alexandria, having been chased all day by country folk wielding pitchforks, sticks, baseball bats and stones."

More thrilling details of this adventure are chronicled in a 12-page article, "Great Northern Virginia Elephant Hunt or The Pachyderm Panic of 1906", The Northern Virginia Review, 2012.[141]

On April 15, 1915, near a trail that Charley and I often take to climb the Ridge to Fort Scott Park, sparks from a fire in the nearby woods caused the signature roller coaster to burn. The park closed and was dismantled that year. Some remains were said to be still visible up to 1988, but all that is now within the high chain link fences of the sewage treatment plant (figure 118). However, after Charley and I climb the steep wooded trail to Fort Scott Park, we look down and imagine what stood there over 100 years ago.

Date written: 9/8/15 revise 1/5/2020
Printed with edit/modification: The Arlington Historical Magazine, Vol 15 No 4, 2016 page 44

Afterward

In 2017 I wrote the first edition of "Walks with Charley: Sniffing Arlington Ridge History and Mystery." Charley, my daily walking companion and best friend and I walk many many miles a year in the Arlington Ridge area and have explored many interesting and unknown stories about the area. In 2020 we are still exploring. Figure 120 is a copy of figure 6 that appears in the "On the Street Where You Live – Arlington Ridge" story of this book. Star annotations mark the stories in this book with numbers identifying the stories starting with "1" for "Charley Girl" and ending with "26" for "From Trolley Park to Sewage Treatment: Luna Park". Star numbering with corresponding stories is shown in Figure 122.

I numbered the stars in the order of stories of the book to trace the flow of "walks."

I had originally intended to write a sequel to "Walks with Charley" and title it "Walks with Dad". I wanted Charley to do more work and become the narrator.

One of my favorite books is "The Art of Racing in the Rain" by Garth Stein. Rather than a human narrator, the narrator is Enzo, the dog. In the book the author makes the case for dogs being the closest relative to humans, not monkeys, as follows:

> "I'll give you a theory: Man's closest relative is not the chimpanzee, as the TV people believe, but is, in fact, the dog..."[142]

Regardless, the concept of having a dog be the narrator in a book was intriguing...and far more challenging than I had expected.

According a recent article in Scientific American:

> "Scientists have made some progress ...They've learned why dogs, and other animals, have rather poor pronunciation and, for example, completely botch consonants. They "don't use their tongues and lips very well, and that makes it difficult for them to match many of the sounds that their human partners make...Try saying 'puppy' without using your lips and tongue..."[143]

I choose to think my Charley is as smart and talented as Enzo, so this book was to be a shared adventure from Charley's perspective.

Charley is not a barker; she is a talker. She only barks to alert us that the someone is at the door. She appears to try to talk to me in low tones, so I believe she knows what she wants to say. She does communicate to me, however, in her own way, and that is sufficient for me to get ideas for stories.

Regardless of how you might read the book, each story was written to stand on its own. Also, my intent was to provide a historical reference for information that has received little attention in the past, but that people wonder about. The book, based on response from the first edition is designed to complement walking tours of our neighborhood, The Ridge. Stories in the book are not numbered like chapters since I believe the book doesn't need to be read in a serial manner. However, the stories are sequenced to generally align with various walks as part of an ENCORE Learning course I teach entitled "Walks with Charley." The course consists of five walking tours (mostly flat) covering Arlington Ridge area (first 4 starting at Hume School and #5 starting at Army Navy Country Club parking lot), as follows:

- Walk 1, Arlington Ridge, Northwest, 2 miles, (General Orientation of area, Hume School, Little Tea House, Fort Albany, Prospect Hill Manor, JEB Stuart Homes, Pentagon Ridge Condos, Sears Bungalows)
- Walk 2, Arlington Ridge, Southeast, 2 miles (Street naming/renaming, Tudors of Arlington, Summer Rentals Offices, "Ty Bryn" & Haley Park, Garfield Estates, Fort Scott, Luna Park)
- Walk 3, Arlington Ridge, Southwest, 2 miles (Arlington Ridge Road, Oak Ridge Elementary School, Gunston Middle School, Shirley Homes, Green Valley Manor, ARNA Valley, Dolley Madison JHS, Fraser Street (23rd St) & view of Fraser cemetery)
- Walk 4, Arlington Ridge, Northeast, 2 miles, (Addison House, Crystal City, Brick Yards, Sunnyside Farm, Jubal Early Homes)
- Walk 5, Army Navy Country Club, 2 miles (Fraser Cemetery, Civil War Fort Richardson and Convalescent Hospital)

Charley and I thank you for taking the time to read about our shared journey over the last nine years.

Figure 121 Arlington Ridge Area

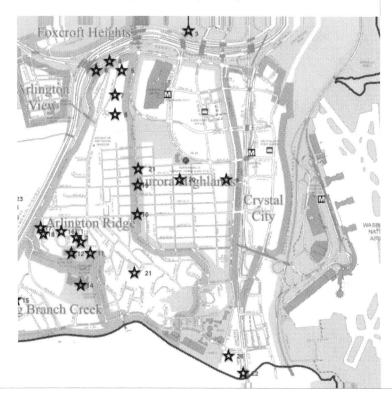

Figure 122 Walks' Story Numbering

Date written: 11/12/2018 revised 1/11/2020

Index

End Notes

[1] Map created by author.

[2] Map, G.M. Hopkins, Atlas of Fifteen Miles Around Washington, DC, 1878, pages 66-77, Library of Congress

[3] Pictures (3) property of author.

[4] Figure, Aurora Highlands Civic Association (AHCA), https://aurorahighlands.org, with permission

[5] Picture, Map Extract from U.S. Coast Survey, Map of Occupation and Defense of the Division of the U.S. Army in Virginia, July 1861, Library of Congress

[6] Picture, Green Valley Manor, Arlington Public Library Center for Local History, Arlington, Virginia with permission.

[7] Nauck: A Community Rich in History, Arlington Historical Society Newsletter, Fall 2013, http://www.arlingtonhistoricalsociety.org/wp-content/uploads/2013/08/AHS-newsletter-9.13-PDF.pdf

[8] Arlington Ridge Road, Wikipedia, http://en.wikipedia.org/wiki/Arlington_Ridge_Road

[9] Wikipedia, Aurora Highlands Historic District, http://en.wikipedia.org/wiki/Aurora_Highlands_Historic_District

[10] Arlington County, Virginia, Street Naming System, http://en.wikipedia.org/wiki/Arlington_County,_Virginia,_street-naming_system Wikipedia

[11] Arlington's Systemic Streets, http://tracktwentynine.blogspot.com/2009/12/arlingtons-systemic-streets.html, December 10, 2009.

[12] Arlington Public Library, Arlington, Virginia; http://library.arlingtonva.us/2013/01/15/do-you-know-what-your-street-used-to-be-named-back-pages/

[13] Library of Congress, Sanborn Fire Insurance Maps; http://www.loc.gov/collections/sanborn-maps/about-this-collection/. Also available in hardcopy at the Arlington County Library, Historical Section

[14] Picture, Pentagon, Google Earth

[15] 1927 Department of Commerce Airway Bulletin

[16] Pictures (composite), Website, http://www.airfields-freeman.com/VA/Airfields_VA_Arlington.htm

[17] Picture, Website, http://www.airfields-freeman.com/VA/Airfields_VA_Arlington.htm

[18] Picture, Harris & Ewing Collection, Library of Congress

[19] Extract of Military Map of NE Virginia, 1865, Map by Engineer Bureau, U.S. War Department, Via Library of Congress, Geography and Map Division - File:1865_Washington.jpg

[20] Extract of Military Map of NE Virginia, 1865, Map by Engineer Bureau, U.S. War Department, Via Library of Congress, Geography and Map Division - File:1865 Washington.jpg

[21] Picture, United States Library of Congress, Prints and Photographs Division, Washington, D.C. 20540 under the digital ID 31297v; Call Number: LOT 4169, no. 33 [P&P] Fort Richardson and Camp of 1st Connecticut Heavy Artillery, https://www.loc.gov/resource/cph.3b16086/

[22] Drawing of Fort Scott, Arlington Public Library Center for Local History, Arlington, Virginia with permission, file folder of miscellaneous artifacts.

[23] Pencil sketch, Harpers Weekly, November 30, 1861

[24] Picture, http://civilwarhome.com/grandreview.html

[25] Picture, Company K, Fort C.F. Smith, August 1865, United States Library of Congress, Prints and Photographs Division; http://cdn.loc.gov/service/pnp/cph/3c10000/3c15000/3c15100/3c15177r.jpg

[26] Figure, Arlington Ridge Area created by author using ARCA Map with permission Arlington Ridge Civil Association.

[27] Picture, Prospect Hill, Washington Evening Star, March 7, 1915, page 59

[28] Sanborn Fire Insurance Maps, 1935 & 1947, Plate 15; Arlington Public Library Center for Local History, Arlington, Virginia, with permission of copyright holder, The Sanborn Library, LLC, c/o Environmental Data Resources, 6 Armstrong Road, 4th Floor, Shelton, CT 06483

[29] Arlington Historical Society Journal, James Roach's Prospect Hill, page 58, 1989.

[30] Picture, Civil War, Fort Albany, Arlington Public Library Center for Local History, Arlington, Virginia with permission; Also, Library of Congress, Prints and Photographs Division, http://cdn.loc.gov/service/pnp/pga/08100/08112r.jpg

[31] ASCE Newsletter, http://www.roadstothefuture.com/VASCE-History/VASCE-Mixing-Bowl.htm, last revised September 25, 1998.

[32] Picture, Little Tea House Well House, c 1923, Arlington Central Library, PG215, with permission.

[33] Picture, Sanborn Fire Insurance Maps, 1935, Plate 17; Arlington Public Library Center for Local History, Arlington, Virginia, with permission of copyright holder, The Sanborn Library, LLC, c/o Environmental Data Resources, 6 Armstrong Road, 4th Floor, Shelton, CT 06483.

[34] Picture, Little Tea House Well House 2016, property of author.

[35] Iron Fireman Magazine (no longer in business) Ad, Little Tea House, Arlington Central Library, PG215, with permission.

[36] Child, Julia, My Life in France, 2006, Page 113.

[37] Pictures, Little Tea House Well House, c 1923, Arlington Central Library, PG215, with permission

[38] ARCA Map with permission Arlington Ridge Civil Association.

[39] Picture, JEB Stuart Homes, Arlington Central Library, with permission.

[40] Sanborn Fire Insurance Maps, 1947, No 15, Arlington Central Library, with permission of copyright holder, The Sanborn Library, LLC, c/o Environmental Data Resources, 6 Armstrong Road, 4th Floor, Shelton, CT 06483.

[41] Pencil sketch created by author of Jubal Early Houses, from picture of unknown origin.

[42] Sanborn Fire Insurance Maps, 1947, No 15, Arlington Central Library, with permission of copyright holder, The Sanborn Library, LLC, c/o Environmental Data Resources, 6 Armstrong Road, 4th Floor, Shelton, CT 06483.

[43] Quote, http://library.arlingtonva.us/2007/05/01/wartime-housing/

[44] Extract of Military Map of NE Virginia, 1865, Map by Engineer Bureau, U.S. War Department, Via Library of Congress, Geography and Map Division - File:1865_Washington.jpg

[45] Sanborn Fire Insurance Map, 1947, No 15, Arlington Central Library, with permission of copyright holder, The Sanborn Library, LLC, c/o Environmental Data Resources, 6 Armstrong Road, 4th Floor, Shelton, CT 06483. Map created by author using extract of ARCA Map with permission Arlington Ridge Civil Association.

[46] Picture, Brickyard near Arlington Ridge, file folder of miscellaneous artifacts, Arlington Public Library Center for Local History, Arlington, Virginia with permission.

[47] Picture, movie theater ad, file folder of miscellaneous artifacts, Arlington Public Library Center for Local History, Arlington, Virginia with permission.

[48] Picture in office of Neighborhood Realty, Arlington Ridge, photographed by Haywood Holland, deceased, and used with permission of his nephew Flavius Hall.

[49] Wikipedia, http://en.wikipedia.org/wiki/Arlington_Ridge_Road

[50] Composite picture of trolley advertisement and map, file folder of miscellaneous artifacts, Arlington Public Library Center for Local History, Arlington, Virginia with permission.

[51] Figure, Arlington Ridge Area created by author using ARCA Map with permission Arlington Ridge Civil Association.

[52] Sanborn Fire Insurance Maps, 1935, No 17; Arlington Public Library Center for Local History, Arlington, Virginia, with permission of copyright holder, The Sanborn Library, LLC, c/o Environmental Data Resources, 6 Armstrong Road, 4th Floor, Shelton, CT 06483.

[53] Pictures (3) of Haley House and Haley children from personal files of Judge Haley used with permission.

[54] Picture. "No Dogs Allowed", property of author.

[55] Picture, Hume School, file folder of miscellaneous artifacts, Arlington Public Library Center for Local History, Arlington, Virginia with permission.

[56] Picture, Charley – Evading "No Dogs", property of author.

[57] Picture, Dolley Madison Junior High School, Green Hornet Yearbook, 1949, Cover, taken by author.

[58] Sanborn Fire Insurance Maps, 1947, No 31, Arlington Central Library, with permission of copyright holder, Environmental Data Resources, P.O. Box 414176, Boston, MA 02241-4176.

[59] Sanborn Fire Insurance Maps, 1947, No 31, Arlington Central Library, with permission of copyright holder, The Sanborn Library, LLC, c/o Environmental Data Resources, 6 Armstrong Road, 4th Floor, Shelton, CT 06483.

[60] Picture, Dolley Madison Towers, owned by author.

[61] Sanborn Fire Insurance Maps, 1952, No 31. Arlington Central Library, with permission of copyright holder, The Sanborn Library, LLC, c/o Environmental Data Resources, 6 Armstrong Road, 4th Floor, Shelton, CT 06483.

[62] http://library.arlingtonva.us/2007/05/01/wartime-housing/

[63] Picture, Gunston Junior High School 1969, Arlington Public Library Center for Local History, Arlington, Virginia with permission, file folder of miscellaneous artifacts.

[64] Picture, Gunston Middle School Rearview and Recreation Fields, property of author.

[65] Sanborn Fire Insurance Maps, 1947, No 31. Arlington Central Library, with permission of copyright holder, The Sanborn Map Sketch Library, LLC, c/o Environmental Data Resources, 6 Armstrong Road, 4th Floor, Shelton, CT 06483; ARCA Map with permission Arlington Ridge Civil Association.

[66] Picture, Arna Valley Apartments, owned by author.

[67] Picture, Arna Valley Apartments, http://images.apartmenthomeliving.com/VA/Arlington/2023267/150904/Arna-Valley-Apartments-Arlington-VA-photo-02_sm.jpg

[68] Washington Post, As the Last Evicted Tenants of Arna Valley Pack Their Things and Leave, They Mourn Their Old Neighborhood--and Worry About Making Ends Meet, Philip P. Pan Monday, December 20, 1999; Page B01

[69] http://www.dhr.virginia.gov/registers/Counties/Arlington/000-9706_Aurora_Highlands_HD_2008_NRfinal.pdf

[70] US Department of Interior, National Park Service, National Places; http://www.dhr.virginia.gov/registers/Counties/Arlington/000-9706_Aurora_Highlands_HD_2008_NRfinal.pdf, Section 7, page 8.

[71] Picture, 2336 S. Nash Street, property of author.

[72] Sanborn Fire Insurance Maps, 1947, No 31. Arlington Central Library, with permission of copyright holder, The Sanborn Library, LLC, c/o Environmental Data Resources, 6 Armstrong Road, 4th Floor, Shelton, CT 06483.

[73] Building Card,
https://archives.arlingtonva.us/publicaccess/PublicAccessProvider.ashx?action=ViewDocument&overlay=Print&overrideFormat=PDF

[74] Sanborn Fire Insurance Maps, 1947, No 31. Arlington Central Library, with permission of copyright holder, The Sanborn Library, LLC, c/o Environmental Data Resources, 6 Armstrong Road, 4th Floor, Shelton, CT 06483.

[75] Morgan collection of Civil War drawings (Library of Congress), Waud, Alfred R. (Alfred Rudolph), 1828-1891, artist; Library of Congress Catalog Number 2004660580

[76] Extract of Civil War map, Library of Congress.

[77] Pictures of Green Valley Manor (two houses, Green Valley Manor, Barn, Spring House), Arlington County Public Library, Pictures Archive (originally from the Columbia Historical Society) with permission.

[78] Extract of article, "With The Rambler", Washington Evening Star, March 7, 1915, page 59.

[79] Mrs. Francis Lee Sickles maintained her maiden name through two marriages – Anderson and Carter

[80] Image, created from Google Earth, no permission required.

[81] Picture, Francis Anderson, Arlington Public Library Center for Local History, Arlington, Virginia with permission.

[82] Figure created by author using ancestry.com

[83] Newspaper clipping, "Historic Barn Burned", Evening Star, Arlington Central Library Center for Local History, PG146, with permission.

[84] Sanborn Fire Insurance Maps, 1947, No 30. Arlington Central Library, with permission of copyright holder, The Sanborn Library, LLC, c/o Environmental Data Resources, 6 Armstrong Road, 4th Floor, Shelton, CT 06483.

[85] Map created by author using extract of ARCA Map with permission Arlington Ridge Civil Association and picture taken by author.

[86] Sketch of the seat of war in Alexandria & Fairfax Cos.,1861, V. P. Corbett; Library of Congress, Maps Division; https://www.loc.gov/resource/g3883a.cw0522000/

[87] Newspaper article excerpt, "With The Rambler", Washington Evening Star, October 7, 1917, page 39

[88] Map Overlay Sketch, Civil War-era markup, Arlington Public Library Center for Local History, Arlington, Virginia with permission.

[89] Advertisement Map, Addison Hills, Arlington Public Library Center for Local History, Arlington, Virginia with permission.

[90] U.S. Federal Census, 1860.

[91] Eleanor Lee Templeton, Arlington Heritage, pg 166.

[92] Sanborn Fire Insurance Maps, 1947, No 30. Arlington Central Library, with permission of copyright holder, The Sanborn Library, LLC, c/o Environmental Data Resources, 6 Armstrong Road, 4th Floor, Shelton, CT 06483.

[93] https://arlingtonva.s3.amazonaws.com/wp-content/uploads/sites/31/2014/03/NC_ArlingtonRidge-Plan_update.pdf

[94] Addison House, 1987 Movie "No Way Out"

[95] Aurora Hills Inset on ARCA Map with permission Arlington Ridge Civil Association.

[96] National Register of Historic Places Registration http://www.dhr.virginia.gov/registers/Counties/Arlington/000-9706_Aurora_Highlands_HD_2008_NRfinal.pdf

[97] Picture, 822 South 20th Street, taken by author.

[98] Picture, 721 South 20th Street, taken by author.

[99] Sunnyside Map Sketch, Arlington County Central Library, Historical Section, with permission.

[100] 1860 Land Book Extract, Arlington County Central Library, Historical Section, with permission.

[101] National Register of Historic Places Registration Form, Aurora Highlands Historic District, VDHR File Number 0000-9706, 2008

[102] Aerial Photographic Map of Arlington County, Virginia; January 11, 1934, Sheet No. 73, Arlington County Central Library, Historical Section, with permission.

[103] Picture, 1807 Arlington Ridge Road, taken by author.

[104] Picture, 1941 Arlington Ridge Road, taken by author.

[105] https://www.lva.virginia.gov/public/guides/opac/lonnabout.htm#patents

[106] Plat, Library of Congress, A plat of the Howson patent, in Arlington County and Alexandria, Virginia from the mouth of the Wampakan Branch near My Lords Island south to the Great Hunting Creek.jpg

[107] Map, Library of Congress, Part of Howsin's Patent in Alexandria Co, Va called 'Green Valley'

[108] During the 1700s and 1800s, Gunter's Chain was the standard for measuring distances and played a primary role in mapping out America. The chain consisted of 100 links and its total length was 4 poles (66 feet). Each link was connected to the next by a round ring. Eighty chains equaled one mile.

[109] https://alextimes.com/2011/09/out-of-the-attic-flooding-is-an-old-pro/

[110] Alexandria Park placard.

[111] Map, Environs of Washington, 1962, Library of Congress.

[112] William Fraser Sr. was sometimes spelled Frazier or Frazer.

[113] Map, Environs of Washington, 1962, Library of Congress;
https://www.loc.gov/resource/g3851s.cw0676000/?r=0.422,0.529,0.284,0.157,0

[114] The 1790 census schedules for Virginia no longer exist as they were burned by the British during the War of 1812. Using state enumerations and tax lists, the 1790 census has been reconstructed for Virginia and published.

[115] US Federal Census, 1840, page 118

[116] US Federal Census, State of Virginia, 1860, page 18

[117] US Federal Census, District of Columbia,1880, Alexandria, 1880, page 22

[118] Photo, Convalescent Camp near Alexandria, Va., May 1863, Library of Congress,
https://www.loc.gov/item/2012650259/

[119] Benjamin Franklin Cooling, III and Walton H. Owen, II, Mr. Lincoln's Forts: A Guide to the Civil War Defenses of Washington (Shippensburg, PA: White Mane Publishing Company, 1988), 81.

[120] Map of the New Convalescent Camp
http://www.13thmass.org/1863/graphics/russell_camp_convalescent.jpg

[121] R.W. Rock (pseudo.), History of the Eleventh Regiment, Rhode Island Volunteers, in the War of the Rebellion (Providence, RI: Providence Press Company, Printers, 1881), 99, 106.

[122] "Barnard map", General Barnard, Chief of Engineers, Defenses of Washington. Maps 1 through 12 accompanying General Barnard's report of the Washington City Fortifications, ESRI. Civil War DC website,
http://civilwardc.org/maps/flex/

[123] Photo, Sanitary Commission Lodge, Convalescent Camp near Alexandria, Va., May 1863, Library of Congress,
https://www.loc.gov/resource/cwpb.01391/

[124] Map, current, ESRI. Civil War DC website, http://civilwardc.org/maps/flex/

[125] http://civilwardc.org/data/places/view/519

[126] Photo, A ward in hospital at convalescent camp near Alexandria, Va., Convalescent Camp near Alexandria, Va, July 1864, Library of Congress, https://www.loc.gov/resource/ppmsca.33646/

[127] The Soldiers' Journal, Library of Virginia's digital newspaper database, Soldiers' Journal, Volume 1, Number 2, 24 February 1864, page 10. https://virginiachronicle.com/?a=d&d=TSJ18640224.1.2&e=-------en-20--1--txt-txIN-------- Printed weekly, for a price of five cents per issue, or two dollars per year, the Soldiers' Journal's eight-page issues included poetry, miscellaneous articles about battles and major war figures, letters from soldiers, camp and personal intelligence, as well as hospital, sanitary, supply, and special relief department directories. Bradley's main agenda with the paper was to educate soldiers about their benefits and to ease them through the wartime bureaucracy. "The soldier in hospital will find in our columns," she wrote, "how to procure pay and clothing when entitled to it; what are the requisites exacted by the Government when furloughs are granted; and discharged soldiers will be put in the way of procuring prompt settlements on their accounts without the interference of claim agents.(Feb. 17, 1864)" During the Journal's short life–it was published from February 1864 to June 1865– its distribution grew to an impressive twenty thousand subscribers, including Abraham Lincoln and Ulysses S. Grant. Finally discontinued in June 1865, the Journal was sold with proceeds from the sale donated to an orphanage.

[128] RG77, Records of Detached Engineer Officers, Defenses of Washington, 1861-66, Entry 556, Registers of Letters Received, 1861-65, Volume 2 organized like a regular Register of Letters Received, page 59-60, C28, Clark, Superintendent, Headquarters, Engineer Camp, Defenses South of the Potomac, October 19, 1863; page 60, C29, C.D. Clark, Superintendent, to A.G. Childs, October 20, 1863; RG393, Preliminary Inventory 172, Part 1, Defenses & Department of Washington, Department and Defenses of Washington and 22nd Army Corps, 1862-69, Entry 5382, Letters Received, September 1862-March 1869, 1863, supplement, Box 2, A31, Alexander to Colonel J.H. Taylor, Chief of Staff, October. 22, 1863.

[129] RG77, Records of Detached Engineer Officers, Defenses of Washington, 1861-66, Entry 556, Registers of Letters Received, 1861-65, Volume 2 organized like a Regular Register of Letters Received, C35, Clark to Childs, November 6, 1863; RG393, Preliminary Inventory 172, Part 1, Department and Defenses of Washington and 22nd Army Corps, 1862-69, Entry 5382, Letters Received, September 1862-March 1869, 1863, supplement, Box 2, A31, Alexander to Colonel J.H. Taylor, Chief of Staff, October 22, 1863; Rock (pseudo.), History of the Eleventh Regiment, 88.

[130] Document, Anthony Fraser Tract, Arlington Central Library, Virginia Historical Section, with permission

[131] Ibid

[132] Ibid Templeton, Eleanor Lee, Arlington Heritage, 1959, page 60.

[133] Arlington County, Virginia Title Company Map, 1900 Alexandria County, Virginia, 1900
http://arlgis.maps.arcgis.com/apps/StorytellingSwipe/index.html

[134] Newspaper article, The Washington Post, June 6, 1927, page 3.

[135] Pictures, Forest Hills Townhomes Construction, Forest Hills Home Owners Association, http://www.foresthillstownhomes.com/photo-archive.html

[136] Picture, Google Earth, no permission required.

[137] Water Treatment Plant aerial photo, Arlington County; Image, created from Google Earth, no permission required.

[138] Washington Luna Park Picture, Arlington Public Library Center for Local History, Arlington, Virginia with permission.

[139] "Plans Are Completed for Luna Park Opening," Washington Times, May 28, 1906.

[140] Luna Park Map sketch, Arlington County Central Library, Historical Section, VA/MAP 975.5296 S7 SANBO 1907 #25 with permission.

[141] Website, http://blogs.nvcc.edu/wp-content/themes/tnvr/mcclellan-raybuck-elephant-hunt.pdf

[142] Stein, Garth, The Art of Racing in the Rain, page 19

[143] Adler, Tina, Scientific American, Fact or Fiction: Dogs Can Talk, June 10, 2009

Made in the USA
Columbia, SC
04 March 2020